Thank You Very Much

a play in two acts by
CECIL P. TAYLOR

in collaboration with
The Northumberland
Experimental Youth Theatre.

ᑎᑎ

Methuen Educational Ltd
London · Toronto · Sydney · Wellington

for SUSAN and MAURICE GILMOUR

First published 1970 by Methuen Educational Ltd
11 New Fetter Lane, London EC4
© 1970 C.P. Taylor
Printed in Great Britain by
Redwood Press Ltd, Trowbridge, Wiltshire
423 44140 X net edition
423 80290 9 school edition

Contents

Foreword

In 1963 the time seemed appropriate for starting a drama group on a County wide basis drawn from exceptionally interested young people. In the event, distance limited membership to a radius of about twenty miles from Newcastle, where the group has met for never less than one evening a week ever since. It seemed we had been right in our judgement, for there was an overwhelming response from young people wanting to join. After intensive auditions we selected thirty, aged between 15 and 20 and it remains at this strength and age range today. Not the same thirty of course, because we have a fairly large turnover each year. They leave to train as teachers, actors, dancers; to become pop singers, clerks, salesmen, postmen, welfare workers or to do voluntary service overseas. Some re-join, many come back to group meetings to renew friendships.

The regime of training is intensive and based on the best kind of educational drama teaching in dance, movement and improvisation. Every major production is prefaced by a full week's residential meeting when each day begins at 8.00 a.m. and frequently goes on till midnight or after. This puts the finish on their work which distinguishes it from less fortunate groups.

Sometimes it seems the word 'experimental' weighs very heavily on the group, but by and large, the description fits. They have presented a 'pop' 'Midsummer Nights Dream', a 'movement' 'Hamlet', and a very earthy, original of course, folk play. In 'After the Donkeys' they made passionate comment on the in-between the Wars period. Their play 'Shadow on the Sun' was the preface to the better known 'Royal Hunt of the Sun'. They put the verbal magic of 'Under Milk Wood' into the merriest, maddest visual setting they have ever perhaps experienced. They were well prepared before doing so. In 'Once Below a Time', the group performed a deeply moving documentary on the life and work of Dylan Thomas. The subsequent production of 'Under Milk Wood' was vibrant with insight and sympathy. Methods of presentation have been in the round, avenue, horseshoe and the proscenium, to name a few.

Most of our new plays started as group improvisations.
The final presentations were highly polished. But we
felt the language of these plays left something to be de-
sired, they lacked shape, and we were not sufficiently
developing character. We needed someone whose trade
was words and the use of them. In short we wanted to
work with a playwright. In 1968 from fifty enquiries and
twenty four firm applications from all over the English
speaking world, including some names with very high
reputations, we appointed Cecil Taylor, who lived on
our doorstep, to a three months fellowship with the
group beginning in May of 1968. In monetary terms it
was equivalent to a University Fellowship.

Three months and a whole world of experience later, we
presented the results of our collaboration with Cecil
Taylor in the shape of 'Thank You Very Much', a play
about a family and their lives as affected by events
leading to the First World War.

Cecil Taylor is still retained by the group as playwright
adviser and other plays have followed as a result of
our joint endeavours.

'Thank You Very Much' as finally written and performed,
moved and excited large audiences. We would like to
recommend it to you.

SILAS HARVEY
Drama Adviser, County of Northumberland
Chairman, Northumberland Experimental Youth Theatre

Introduction

MAKING THE PLAY

There is some intangible skill in writing a play which makes it one of the most hazardous communication media. It is not like riding a bike, where once you acquire the knack you never lose it. Every time I sit down to start a new play I am overwhelmed with feelings of insecurity and uncertainty, and the grounds for those feelings are only confirmed as I go into the play, move three steps backwards and one forwards and take wrong turning after wrong turning. Only after this fool's course do I eventually see what the play I'm writing is about, which course it <u>should</u> take and how it should be shaped.

I am setting down the path THANK YOU VERY MUCH took in the hope that it might be helpful to writers and others creating new plays for Youth theatre. It might be reassuring to some that at least one writer shares with them the disturbing feeling of not knowing where he is going until he is there.

The process of the writing of THANK YOU VERY MUCH was a gradual scaling down of ambition. It was 'sold' to the Experimental Youth Theatre – the first hurdle to be cleared in Youth theatre, of course, is to 'sell' the idea of the play to the people who will be creating it – as a play entitled BIRTHS DEATHS AND MARRIAGES. This was going to be a huge epic, dealing with the changing attitudes to love, birth, death, Socialism, war and everything else you can think of. It was going to range through three generations and deal with the outbreak of two wars, World War One and Two, and the near outbreak of World War Three, during the Cuba Crisis.

With just three months to work on the play, some ten Friday evenings of two hours and a week's residential course for actual work with the group, the original outline was clearly stretching everyones talents and resources. We scaled down the ambition a degree, and limited the play to dealing with the first section of BIRTH DEATHS AND MARRIAGES – the days leading to the outbreak of World War One.

I then produced sheet after sheet of data, about the historical events of the twenty years leading to 1914, about contemporary fashions, entertainment, social history, outlines of the characters in the play, and the group began a series of improvisations based on these data sheets while I wrote the first draft of THANK YOU VERY MUCH. This, in fact, was two plays, a study of the personality interactions which led to the outbreak of the first world war and a study of the effect of these interactions on the ordinary people of Newcastle. We went into rehearsal with this double play.

While I had used the actual words of the leading political characters of the day, such was the tone of the times and the marked individuality if not eccentricity of these characters, that putting their words down in cold blood, without any distortion on my part, was sheer satirical comedy. It soon became clear that the one play was pulling against the other and cancelling the whole show into a dramatic vacuum.

One afternoon, after days of moving round in circles, during one of the family scenes, somebody played a quiet roll on a tympani we had in the hall. It suddenly became clear to me what was wrong with this double play. The function of the political scenes was to give the effect of a mounting threat over the people of Newcastle, an ever darkening shadow, growing all the time and approaching nearer and nearer till it darkens the lives of the characters in the play.

We now knew exactly where we were going, because we were there.

THE LANGUAGE OF THE PLAY

This play is set on Tyneside simply because local sources were convenient to hand and I had thirty-odd players who were at home with the dialect.

However, only a few of the characters speak the Tyneside dialect. The rest, while using the 'tune' of the North East, use the 'good English' of the artisans and shopkeepers throughout the country. The play is designed to be adapted - and I hope it will be - to any regional production.

The only two words in the play which may present difficulties are 'divvent' which means 'don't' and 'gannin' which means 'going'.

THE ASSASSINATION AT SARAJEVO

Sarajevo was the principal city in Bosnia – now Jugo-slavia – a Slav country occupied at the time by Austria, as part of her foreign policy of keeping the Slavs divided and holding back the inevitable decay of her own empire.

On June 28th, 1914, The Archduke Ferdinand, heir to the Austrian throne, was assassinated while reviewing the troops at Sarajevo, by Serbian assassins.

The Austrians, because of the complicated mesh of treaties which involved Serbia with Russia, France and Great Britain, had to tread very carefully at the initial stages of their plot to use the assassination as a pre-text for an attack on Serbia, and initiate the final phase of her subjugation of the Slavs. Kaiser William was the key figure at this crucial stage. With his support, they could go ahead with the plot, confident that no nation would challenge the united power of Austria and Germany.

On Sunday, July 5th, 1914, Kaiser William authorised the Austrian Ambassador in Germany to convey to Vienna that 'The Austrian Emperor could reckon on the full support of Germany'. 'His Majesty said,' the report to Vienna ran, 'He understood how hard Francis Joseph with his well known love for peace would find it to invade Serbia'. But if Austria decided that military action against Serbia was necessary, he would be sorry if they left the present moment which was so favourable to us, unused.'

William had set the machinery in motion. By August 5th, 1914, all Europe was at war.

STAGING THE PLAY

The play was staged in two areas – a raised stage
and an acting area on the floor. The political pro-
logues and epilogues were played on the stage while
the family scenes were played on the floor. The music-
hall scenes moved freely from stage to floor, the
family sometimes joining in the music-hall events.

In the original productions, the play opened with the
group entering the auditorium in their contemporary
clothes, carrying their costumes. They exchanged
items of costume, saying 'Thank You Very Much',
repeating this until it became a loud chant. They then
moved into the Scaffold version of THANK U VERY
MUCH, as they changed into costume. Once they were
all in costume, the music changed to the 1914 version
of THANK YOU VERY MUCH and the play began.

The final script is based on two highly inventive
productions of the play by Northumberland Experimental
Youth Theatre. The core of the play is in the family
story and the individual director is free to stage this
story according to his concepts and the practical resources of his theatre.

C.P.T.

STAGE PLAN AND DESIGN NOTES

These are from the original production, designed by Emlyn Evans.

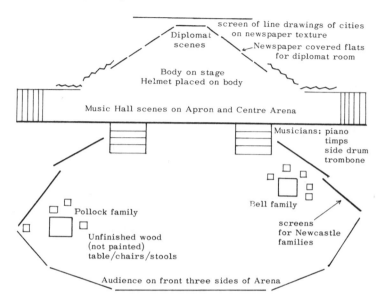

Contrast between diplomats and families

Flats for families: hessian with line drawings of Newcastle and area.
Flats for diplomats: newspaper collage, with line drawings to typify cities involved.

Lighting: Diplomat scenes – steel blue/frost Family scenes – straw/chocolate Music hall – open white/rose/light salmon

CHARACTERS IN THE PLAY

MORAY BELL	–	Commercial traveller
MARGARET	–	His wife
FRANCIS	–	His sister
ANNIE	–	His sister
RAY	–	His sister
GEORGE	–	Annie's husband
WALTER	–	Margaret's brother
RALPH	–	Francis's husband
FLORRIE POLLOCK	–	Typist, suffragette
STAN	–	Her father
MARY	–	Her mother
MAY	–	Her sister
ROSE	–	Her sister
MR NORRIE		

PALACE OF VARIETIES CHARACTERS

POLLY BURTON	–	fresh from her London triumph

1st and 2nd Comedians

THE WAR MAKERS

THE EMPEROR FRANZ JOSEPH

THE KAISER

VIVIANI

SASSANOV

GREY

The thirteen items in the play should be indicated, if possible, by an illuminated number-plate at the side of the stage, as in the old Palace of Varieties.

ACT ONE

Prologue

Black stage. A shot is fired. Lights on the KAISER
and the AUSTRIAN EMPEROR standing over the body
of the ARCHDUKE FERDINAND.

KAISER: This cowardly crime, this unutterable mis-
fortune! It has shaken me to the very depths of
my soul!

EMPEROR: The assassination of my poor nephew and
the heir to the Austrian throne by Serbian fanatics
is the climax of the agitation of Russian and Serbian
Pan Slavs.

KAISER (turning to the EMPEROR): Only fourteen days
ago, I was with him and his dear wife, Sophie, and
his darling children!

EMPEROR: By their agitation for Serbia to abandon her
present happy relations with Austria and move into
an alliance with the Slavs, their single aim is the
weakening and disruption of the Austrian Empire.

KAISER (over the body): God comfort the Archduke's
unfortunate children. (Turning to the EMPEROR)
And God comfort you, Your Imperial Majesty Franz
Joseph!

EMPEROR: Serbia is the pivot of the Slav policy to
destroy my dynasty and rob me of my territories.
She must be eliminated, William, as a political
factor in the Balkans.

KAISER: Your Imperial Majesty, you can count on
Germany's full support. Whatever you may decide –
whether to invade Serbia or take some other military
action against her. Austria can count with cer-
tainty that Germany will stand by her friend and
Ally...

(They shake hands over the body. Lights up on the
Music Hall and into the play.)

1   <u>THANK YOU VERY MUCH</u>

Palace of Varieties. A Friday night. The characters
in the play are seated on either side of the stage. The
opening number on the bill has just started. POLLY
BURTON is just beginning the chorus.

'THANK YOU VERY MUCH'

POLLY:
    A little boy sat on his Mummy's knee
    And said: 'Mummy, please teach me to pray.
    I want to learn to speak to God
    And please him in every way'.
    The mother smiled an angel's smile,
    And patted his golden head.
    She squeezed his hand
    And kissed his cheek
    And this is what she said:
    She said: (All together, now...)

CHORUS:
    Thank you...Thank you...Thank you,

    How deep these few words can touch
    The heart of your Friend and your Maker,
    Thank you very much.

POLLY:
    Although your Daddy's in heaven, now,
    Holding your sister's hand,
    And brother Tim is sinking fast,
    You must understand.
    God is very busy, dear.
    We must be content with our lot.
    We're just passing through,
    All he wants us to do,
    Is thank him for what we've got.

    Just say:
    Thank you, etc. (Cheers. Applause):...'More!
    More!'

    (Orchestra plays singer off the stage...and into
    Scene One.)

Scene One

The parlour of Moray Bell's house. The family have gathered to put pressure on Moray to christen his first son 'Moray', and continue the family tradition.

FRANCIS, a pad on her lap, is composing the announcement of the birth. RAY is beside her, backing her up, as usual, to the hilt.

MARGARET is nursing the baby. WALTER is at the closed piano, now and then, when an idea occurs to him, trying it out on the lid.

ANNIE is seated beside GEORGE, who is reading one of Moray's left-wing periodicals. MORAY himself is busy, preparing for a demonstration against the recent National Insurance Act. He is working on a poster: 'National Insurance – Daylight Robbery Act!'

FRANCIS (reading what she has written so far): Bell. At 15, Cromwell Street, Elswick, Newcastle-on-Tyne. To Moray and Margaret (nee Hunter) a son, Moray. Sincere thanks to Dr Alan –

MORAY (correcting her): Thomas!

FRANCIS (with disgust): Tommy!

RAY: Tommy, Moray!

FRANCIS: What kind of name is that for the son of a Commercial Traveller!

MORAY: Tommy.

ANNIE (to MARGARET): Is that what you fancy for him, Margaret...(Going over to admire the baby) Ee! He's such a lovely lad!

GEORGE (looking up from his magazine): This Archduke Ferdinand chap that got himself shot...Ye knaa he wasn't married to his wife?

FRANCIS (turning on MARGARET): Margaret! I thought you were all for keeping the family tradition and calling him 'Moray'.

RAY. She was! The other day she was all for 'Moray'!

MARGARET: Aa didn't say Aa was all for callin' him 'Moray', Ray. Aa just said, Aa could see the family's point of view.

GEORGE: Aa divvent think much of a chap that gans and gets all them children with a woman he hasn't had the decency to marry!

ANNIE: Eee, Georgie, I wish you wouldn't talk about these things! You don't talk about things like that in company...

GEORGE: He bloody deserved to be shot! Gettin' all them children with a woman he wasn't married to!

MORAY: Looka! He could've had a bloody harem and they could've all been mowed down by machine-guns and the Austrians wouldn't have turned a bloody hair if it suited them. They're not worried about the Archduke being shot, man! It's just an excuse to take over Serbia!

GEORGE: Looka, man! Aa read it in the bloody papers! In black and bloody white! They weren't married... All the royalty never used to speak to her...She never got invited anywhere...

MORAY: Never mind the bloody duke, man! What about this name for me lad? Isn't that a good fighting name for him, George? 'Tommy'. After one of the founders of the Miners' Union...Tommy Hepburn...

GEORGE: What the hell's Tommy Hepburn got to do with yer bairn's christenin'? Ye're not a bloody miner. Ye're a traveller...Ye're a commercial bloody traveller...Never done a day's stroke in yer life, Moray, man!

FRANCIS (turning to WALTER as a possible ally. WALTER is busy at the piano lid. She catches him in the middle of a run in the bass): Walter, have you nothing to say about this break with the family tradition...

RAY (quickly backing her up): You should have <u>something</u> to say about it, Walter! It's your sister's boy!

(WALTER looks up, frightened. He looks at MARGARET, but she is nursing the baby. The two sisters are staring at him, waiting for him to say something.)

WALTER: Aa haven't thought about it much, like...

FRANCIS: You haven't thought about it!

RAY: You haven't thought about the christening of your only sister's first boy!

WALTER: What Aa mean to say, is...Aa've thought about it...But...But...This 'Terror In the Air' Picture, we're doin' next week, Fanny...It's got us all worked up, Fanny!

MARGARET: It's got him all worked up to the nineties, Fanny.

WALTER: It's about them aeroplanes...There's a war. And they fly over the towns and drop bombs. And fight in the air.

MARGARET: He's having a terrible time getting the right music.

WALTER: You're up and down the piano, up and down, all the time...(FRANCIS is no longer listening to him. She has dismissed him as totally useless for her campaign. She turns back to MORAY) Mostly on the heavy notes for the bombs...

FRANCIS: You're quite happy then, Moray Bell. To call the first son in the family after a pitman.

RAY: That'll be his ambition for the poor child. To send him down the pits. I wouldn't put it past him!

ANNIE: He could be called after a lot worse than a pit-man! The way the pair of you are talking...

GEORGE: Na, man...Aa knaa what they're talkin' aboot...If we had a lad...Aa'd never send him down the pit, Annie, man...

ANNIE: Eee! If we had a baby to be christened Georgie! Aa wouldn't know what to do. I'd be happy to call him anything!

MARGARET: We are going to have a proper christening, Moray, aren't we?

(MORAY is about to say something – but FRANCIS forestalls him.)

FRANCIS: I'll make sure he has! I've some rights as the eldest in the family!

RAY: Even if we have to get him to the church at pistol-point!

ANNIE: Bank Holiday Sunday would've been lovely –

there's something nice about a Bank Holiday Sunday
Christening...

MORAY: It's too soon, man! I've got the kitchen still to
paint...

MARGARET: Eee...Aa wish ye'd change that paint,
Moray...He's going to paint the whole kitchen green!

MORAY: Leaf green, man.

MARGARET: You know Aa've got me ways about green,
Moray...Me mother would never have green in the
house...

GEORGE: Aa like a red...A nice bright red...Ye can't
beat a red!

ANNIE: I think it would've been lovely, an August Bank
Holiday christening...

FRANCIS: It's no use going into Bank Holiday Sunday
again, Annie! Reverend Harrison's booked. He's
fully booked for Bank Holiday Sunday...

MARGARET: And Moray's going to London for a meeting...

FRANCIS: We'd've soon stopped him going to London, if
Reverend Harrison hadn't been booked.

MORAY: Looka...Why don't you give us up? I'm no use
to you...I'm a disgrace to the family!

ANNIE: Moray...You're our own brother...Moray...
How could we give you up...Your own flesh and
blood, Moray...

FRANCIS: That would just suit you, wouldn't it, Moray
Bell. That would be just up your alley...Just to
be left to run wild and please yourself...You listen
to me, Moray Bell. You're the head of the family,
now...And don't think we're going to let you run
away from your responsibilities...

MORAY: No...I'll resign, Fanny, man...And you can
take over...

GEORGE (to FRANCIS): There's a canny job for ye,
Fanny!

(As they have been speaking, WALTER has been
wrestling with a problem. Suddenly he articulates
it.)

WALTER: Why has it to be 'Moray'? Why has it always
to be 'Moray'?

MAGGIE: It's a Bell tradition, Walter.

RAY: It's a family tradition. There's always been a
    Moray in the family.

ANNIE: The first lad born into the family's always
    called 'Moray'.

WALTER (not very much the wiser): There's always
    been a Moray Bell, like...

ANNIE: It's a tradition, Walter...

MORAY: It's the clan, man! It's the Clan Moray. You're
    all shooting out your heck for the lad to be called
    'Moray' and you don't even know the meaning of the
    tradition!

GEORGE: Scottish, like...The Clan...

MORAY: The Clan Moray!

FRANCIS: I know it's the Clan Moray. What are you
    shouting about?

MORAY (to GEORGE and WALTER): My great great great
    – God knows bloody when grandfather...He slunk
    over the border after the 1745 rebellion...Into
    Wooler...He was in the Clan Moray.

WALTER: Bonnie Prince Charlie. I played for the
    picture. 'Over the Seas to Skye'...(Begins to hum
    and play the piano lid) Lovely tune...Lovely thing,
    that!

GEORGE: What side was he on?

MORAY: He was on the wrong side. That's another
    tradition of the Bells. We've always been on the
    losing side...Till now...

    That's the idea, George, man...That's why I'm
    putting a stop to Moray! We're on the winning
    side, now...We're going to win...The people are
    on the rise, man...And we're going to win...
    There's not going to be any more wars with workers
    fighting workers...The next war will be Labour
    against Capital...

FRANCIS (standing...suddenly): Wait a minute!

MORAY: That's the only war people will fight now...

FRANCIS: Be quiet a minute, will you. (Listening,
    looking up) Do you feel it, Ray?

    (RAY and ANNIE join her, looking up at the ceiling and
    listening.)

Do you know what it is? It's Father and Mother...
Looking down on us...Just now...

RAY: Eee, Fanny...I had a funny feeling too...

ANNIE: It was like somebody looking at the back of my
neck.

MORAY: From up there? I wish they were. I wish there
was a place up there...And I'd have somewhere to
go to, at the end of it all.

GEORGE: Ye'll never gan up there, ye bugger, man...
Ye'll be lucky if they take ye below...

FRANCIS: Can ye feel it, Ray...

ANNIE: It's like them hanging on to our words...
Waiting for Moray to take the right decision.

MORAY: Are ye there, Da...Mother...

FRANCIS: You've got no feelings, Moray...You've never
had any normal feelings.

RAY: He's always been a callous character...

ANNIE: He's got no heart...

MORAY: Da...Ma...

FRANCIS: I think that's outrageous...That really is...
It's outrageous behaviour...Insulting the dead like
that...

MORAY: Wait a minute, Fanny, man. Give them a chance.
They've a long way to hear us...Ma...Da...

ANNIE: Can nobody stop him.

MORAY: Mother...Father, it's me...Moray...

NARGARET: Moray...stop it...You're making us feel
bad...

FRANCIS: Have you no consideration for your poor
wife...Just out of her childbed.

MORAY: I'm going to call your grandson Tommy, Ma...
Is that alright.

RAY: He gets worse every day. He has no respect for
anybody.

MORAY: What do they do...Do they knock three times
for no and once for yes?

GEORGE: Ye want a megaphone, Moray, man. That's
what ye need to get through to them...

MORAY: Ma...Da...

FRANCIS (getting up): If you're going to carry on like this, Moray Bell, I'm not going to stay here one minute longer.

GEORGE: Tell ye what...That old British word...What de ye call it again...Moray? Neither the one thing nor the other...

ANNIE: George...Will you stop interfering.

GEORGE: Man, Aa'm trying to get agreement, man. In between, neither flesh nor fowl.

MORAY: Compromise.

GEORGE: That's the word, Moray! Compromise...The family wants Moray...Moray wants Tommy...Call him Tommy Moray Bell.

FRANCIS: Moray Thomas Bell.

GEORGE: What de ye say, Moray, man...We could be standin' arguin' here till the bairn's on the way to his bloody wedding!

MORAY: Moray Tom for his christening...But we call him, Tommy Moray.

FRANCIS: That's settled, then, Moray? 'Moray Thomas' for his christening?

MORAY: I told you, man! (Gathering up his leaflets and his poster for the demonstration)

RAY: Thank God that's settled, at last!

FRANCIS (reading out the new announcement): Bell, at 15, Cromwell Street...Elswick, Newcastle –

MORAY (going): You work it all out with Maggie, Fanny...I've got to get to the Bigg Market...To burn the National Insurance Act...

(He marches out with his poster over his shoulder.)

<u>END OF SCENE</u>

DAUGHTER (just going): Daddy, you will be nice to Gerald when he comes to ask for my hand, tonight, won't you?

FATHER: It's a bit awkward him coming the same night as this chap coming to buy me greyhound. He'd better not stay too long. And if the chap turns up to see Pride and Joy – he'll just have to go sharp ...that's all.

DAUGHTER (kissing him on the brow and going): Be nice to him, Daddy.

FATHER (muttering to himself): I've got her nicely brushed...clean straw in her kennel...yes... brushed her teeth...

(As he is talking to himself GERALD, the suitor, nervously pokes his head through the door.)

GERALD: Good evening, sir.

FATHER: 'Ullo...You came about me Pride and Joy...

GERALD: Yes, sir...

FATHER: I'd never've thought of parting with her. But I've another six, now.

GERALD: Six, sir! Sisters?

FATHER: Not exactly sisters, like. They had the same father. But different mothers.

GERALD: Oh...I see. Yes.

FATHER: I don't do it for the money, you know.

GERALD: I'm sure you don't. No...

FATHER: I could get thousands out of them, if I kept them to meself. But I just like bringing them on till they're ready to tackle the world...Then I'm happy to see them go to the right man who knows a good thing when he sees one. You know a good thing when you see one, I can see that.

GERALD: Yes. I do...Very much...

FATHER: Yes...I can see you've a bit of an eye for the Pride and Joys...Eh...(Nudging him)

GERALD: Just this particular one, sir.

FATHER: You haven't had any before?

GERALD (shocked): Oh, no...Sir...Definitely not...
Never...

FATHER: Well...You've got to make a start sometimes.
I suppose everybody can't be like me...I had me
first one when I was twelve...My father gave me her.

GERALD: Your father –

FATHER: Of course, he had dozens in his lifetime.
Hundreds! Taught me all there is to know about
them. You'll look after her alright...Will you...I
wouldn't like to think she wasn't going to be well
looked after.

GERALD: I have a very good position, sir. I'm going
to buy a new house with every modern convenience and –

FATHER: I wouldn't go to all that bother. Just give
her a nice bed of straw and she's happy as a queen!
You want to change the straw regular, mind...
She's clean enough...But after a bit...It does get
to smell.

GERALD: Sir...Only the finest bed linen would be
good enough for her.

FATHER: You do throw your money around, don't
you! Oh...About her meat...She doesn't like it
cooked...She likes nothing better than a raw heart
or a nice pair of lungs...Doesn't matter if it's a
bit off...All the better...She prefers it...And when
you bath her...Just tickle her tummy to get her in a
good mood...She likes that...Once she gets in the
water, she enjoys herself, alright!

GERALD: Are you still...

FATHER: We have a right old time of it, we do! Talk
about fun and games in the bath! Well...Shall we
get her and take her into the field and let her frolic
around a bit?

GERALD: Well, sir, if she wouldn't object...

FATHER: You want to see what she can do before you
take her don't you? You don't want to be buying a
pig in a poke...You want to give her a proper try-
out...to be sure you're going to get satisfaction for
your money...

(As he is talking the DOG BUYER enters.)

BUYER: 'Ullo...Come about your dog. Pride and Joy...

FATHER: Another one! I've got this gent here, waiting to buy her...

GERALD: Sir! Is that what you've been talking about, all this time. Your dog, Pride and Joy?

FATHER (turning on him): What do you think I've been talking about?

GERALD: We've been talking about your dog, sir. Pride and Joy!

(Blackout)

Scene Two SATURDAY, 25th JULY, 1914

Florrie's house. Early evening.

ROSE and MAY are cutting out a dress-pattern. STAN is by the fire, carving. FLORRIE is taking off her outdoor things, having just come in...

STAN (to FLORRIE): Aa didn't raise me voice to her, Florrie. Ask May and Rose. Did Aa?

BOTH (bored with the topic): No. You didn't, Da...

ROSE (trying to forestall a long story from STAN): Me Mam made a steak pie...

STAN: It wasn't the steak pie, Rose, man...The steak pie was over...We'd finished, talkin' about the pie ...It was me suit...

MAY: Me Ma pawned me Dad's best suit...

FLORRIE: For something for the house, again?

STAN: Aa just said to her. Very calm, like, Florrie... Looka: It's a bit much you pawnin' me best suit to buy new curtains and me havin' to gan te me work with nowt but bread and drippin' on me bread, day in day out...

ROSE (trying to stop STAN): You're late back, Florrie ...Have you been to one of your meetings, again?

STAN: It's a curse, man! This mania she's got for changing about the house! Aa've never had me suit in the pawn in me life!

MAY: Eee, have you seen our Florrie making one of her speeches, Da? You should see her! She gets up on the platform...

ROSE and MAY: Votes for women! Votes for women!

STAN: Aa divvent like it, out in a strange place, Florrie ...Strangers handling it...

FLORRIE: We'll get it out for you on Friday, Da... Don't upset yourself about it...

MAY: She gets up on a platform, with all the men around her...

STAN: It's really upset us, Florrie, man...it gives me a funny feeling...

ROSE: I think she likes all the men's eyes on her...

STAN: Watch your tongue, Rose, man, will you!

FLORRIE: That's right. I like it. I like all the men watching us!

STAN: Florrie, man! Watch your talk, will you!

FLORRIE (watching him): Isn't it funny, Da...You can never leave off your carving. You carve all day at the factory...And when you get home at night –

STAN: That's work, man! I'm carvin' sideboards and dressing tables an' that. This is animals...Looka ...You recognise it?

ROSE: It's a dog.

FLORRIE: It's a greyhound. It's lovely, Da...

STAN: It's your Uncle Charlie's greyhound. You not recognise the face?

FLORRIE: It's lovely, Da...It's very good! You've got its muscles and everything. Just like real, Da... Ee...You'd just think it was going to spring up and tear off down the track!

STAN: Aa drawed him while your Uncle Charlie fed him hearts...Went through two big hearts till Aa got him right...

FLORRIE (on a didactic tack, now): Da...if you made nothing but dogs and horses and that...Wouldn't you make more a week than in the factory?

STAN: Who wants them lass?

MAY: You could take a stall on the Quayside, Da...

FLORRIE: Some of the things you carve, Da...They're beautiful!

ROSE: I liked Tibby, Da...Didn't he do Tibby, canny?

STAN: She's a lovely cat, Tibby...A perfect specimen of a tabby cat...

FLORRIE: See...That's what I mean, Da...How Capitalism, is so stupid. You could be making all those beautiful things...

STAN: It's an art, man...It's an art...Yer Granda had it a bit...

FLORRIE: But Capitalism thinks your sideboards and wardrobes are worth more than your carving.

MAY: Is that what your Socialism would do, Florrie? Let Da stop in the house all day and carve cats and dogs...

ROSE: Me Mam wouldn't like that would she, Da? You stopping in, all day, carving...

STAN: Aa wouldn't want to stop in the house all day, Florrie...

FLORRIE: You wouldn't work in the house, Da. The State would give you a workshop. We'd get all the worker artists in one big building...A kind of Palace of Arts...

STAN: That would be working, man. It wouldn't be the same...Aa wouldn't have the same spirit for me carvin' if it was working...You see what Aa mean. Aa wouldn't like that...

MAY: What palace would they have for you, Florrie? A Palace of Typewriting?

ROSE: Florrie would have a Palace of Love. Wouldn't you, Florrie? For you and your – (She pretends to check herself) Ee, Florrie! Do you not want me Da to know?

FLORRIE (sharply): You've told him now, anyway... whether I wanted to or not!

ROSE: Well, you don't need to get on to us like that! It just slipped out...

STAN: Ye'd better go and see what ye can do with yer Mam, Florrie...

FLORRIE (to her father): It's just somebody they've seen us walking out with...That's all, Da...

MAY: He's middle-aged looking for you, Florrie, isn't he?

STAN: Let her see to your Mam, May, man!

ROSE: He doesn't dress very smart, does he, Florrie?

MAY: What's his name?

FLORRIE: You should have come straight up to us when you saw us. I would've put you out of your misery and introduced you. His name's Moray...And he sells groceries round the shops for a wholesaler...

ROSE: Oh...He's a <u>businessman</u>!

FLORRIE: He's a Socialist.

MAY: Do you hear that, Da...Our Florrie's walking out with a businessman!

ROSE: Are you going to ask me Mam to let you bring him to tea, Florrie?

FLORRIE: I'll see what happens. If we decide to get married...I'll maybe bring him here on the way to the church. To show him what sister-in-laws he's letting himself in for!

(FLORRIE flounces out).

ROSE: Oh, dear me!

MAY: We're terribly sorry we're not good enough for you!

ROSE: Pity about you!

(FLORRIE goes up to her Mother's bedroom. The lights fade in the kitchen...up in the bedroom.

Florrie's mother's bedroom.

MARY, Florrie's mother, is in bed, listening to FLORRIE approaching, her eyes wide open. She hears the door being opened, she sinks back in her bed and closes her eyes, pretending to be fast asleep. Florrie enters and approaches the bed.)

FLORRIE: Are you alright, Ma? (No answer) Do you want anything, Ma? (No answer) Ma, do you want anything?

MOTHER: Death! Death! That's what I want!

FLORRIE: Will I bring you up a cup of tea, Ma?

MOTHER (sitting up): I am not a Catho-lick! I don't know anything about their feast days and their denial days and their bloody saints days! I told him when I married him. I am C of E and your priests and your bishops can stand on their heads and shoot at me to me dying day, I will stay C of E! (Looking down at the floor to the kitchen) What is he doing down there? (Shouts) Playing with his block of wood and his knife? The house could fall on top of us and we could all perish and he'd still be playing with his block of wood!

FLORRIE: You're not even C of E, Ma. Are you?

MOTHER: It's his nerves. That's what it is. He has to play with his block of wood because of his nerves!

FLORRIE: You've never been inside a church...since I was confirmed!

MOTHER: I'm not well enough. God has seen fit to deny me the strength to regularly visit His House. The spirit is strong.

FLORRIE: Do you know what I think, Ma. I think you're like me. You don't believe in anything.

MOTHER: Did you have any of the pie?

FLORRIE: I haven't had anything yet, Ma.

MOTHER: I should've known better. You never get any thanks from Catholics. Anything good that happens to them comes from the Pope and anything bad from the Protestants. I put down in front of them a steak and onion pie...It was melting in the dish...The gravy was coming out of the golden brown crust. The smell of it! Didn't you smell it when you came in?

FLORRIE: Da says it was his suit. He said you pawned his suit.

MOTHER: You're a queer one, Florrie...You didn't turn out a Catholic like the other two, but you're a queer character, nevertheless...Sometimes I can never fathom you out...I don't know whose friend you are...whose side you're on...

FLORRIE: Sometimes Da's...Sometimes yours. It depends who's in the right, doesn't it, Ma?

MOTHER: No Catholic can be in the right, girl! Their minds are poisoned by their priests and their

Bishops. I put this gold brown, melting steak pie in front of them with boiled potatoes and cabbage... That's after him crying to us. All he gets is bread and dripping...And syrup on Fridays...His face hits the table...I says what the hell is up with you. Your face is hitting the table...Today, he says, is a Denial Day...Some bloody saint of theirs had a drunken fit and fell down a cliff and died. I am not a Catholic, I said, I don't know your feast days and your self-denial days. The two girls were as bad as him. They wouldn't have any, either. Starve, I says. Bloody starve! If that's the way you want it. I've nothing else for you in the house. It's Thursday...Now who's in the right, there?

FLORRIE: I like me Da, Ma...

MOTHER: Let them go to Mass, the three of them and ask the Pope to provide! You like your Da?

FLORRIE: Yes...I like him. He's cannie...

MOTHER: I was lying here, thinking on...What did I see in him? How did I come to marry that.

FLORRIE: You're more interesting, Ma...I like talking to you, better...But I like you both...

MOTHER: God! It's more than he deserves! He never bothered with you when you were young. It was all I could do to get him to take you to the Park on a Sunday. The two Catholics like him better than me. But that's just because they're Catholics.

FLORRIE: I'll bring you up some pie and a cup of tea Ma...

MOTHER: I'm not going to eat me pie up here out of their sight and smell...I'll come down in a minute and have me tea with you...I'll give them a good sight and smell of the pie...We'll finish it off between us!

FLORRIE: I'll go down and put the oven on...

MOTHER (catching her hand. Searching FLORRIE'S face): Let's see you a minute girl.

FLORRIE (embarrassed under the close look): You've seen us before, Ma.

MOTHER: Have you just come in? You finish your work at half past five.

FLORRIE: I was at a meeting.

MOTHER: Do you like the new curtains?

FLORRIE: They're lovely, Ma...

MOTHER: You're happy, these days, love? Aren't you? I've never seen you so happy with yourself before! (Searching her face).

FLORRIE: I'm not all that happy, Ma...

MOTHER: You've got yourself some lad, haven't you, Love?

FLORRIE: I've just walked out with him a few times... that's all, Ma...(Going to avoid any more questions) I'll go and put the kettle on, Ma...

MOTHER: Are you going to bring him up to see us, Florrie?

FLORRIE: I'll see what happens, Ma...Eh?

(Going — but her MOTHER grips her and keeps her at the bed).

MOTHER: Florrie...Don't leave us, surrounded by all them Catholics, will you?

FLORRIE: Don't be daft, Ma...They're your daughters, like me, Ma...

MOTHER (still anxiously searching FLORRIE'S face): They're a lovely quality of curtain...Did you notice the way they hang?

FLORRIE (going): They're lovely, Ma...I'll get the kettle on...

MOTHER (turning to admire the curtains...sighing): Yes ...I'm very happy with them. I am!

<u>END OF SCENE</u>

3 <u>MUSICAL SEX–WAR</u>

The usual musical sex–war is going on. On one side of
the stage a COMEDIAN has the men's printed song behind
him, on the other POLLY has the girls'

COMEDIAN: Tell you what! Tell you what! If you won't
work for us...maybe you'll work for yourselves...
Let's have a lady and a gent from the audience to
conduct the singing. Alright, Polly?

POLLY: If you pick the lady and I pick the gent.

COMEDIAN: Alright, ladies and gentlemen...Any lady
and gent in the audience who fancies themselves as
a conductor...Come on now...Don't be shy...

(They go round the audience. POLLY picks RALPH.
Reluctantly he follows her. The COMEDIAN picks
MAY.)

COMEDIAN: Right...The Boys first...Loud as you
can...Show the girls what we can do...

(They launch into the song.)

SONG:
    You can't beat a glass of Brown Ale,
    It's got a sting from its head to its tail.
    It puts hair on your chest,
    Fire in your chest –
    A nice, tasty glass of Brown Ale.

POLLY: Come on now, Girls...Let's show the boys
really how to sing.

(Into women's song.)

SONG:
    You can't beat a glass of good port,
    It fills you with fun and with sport.
    If you want a complexion,
    That's perfect perfection,
    Have a nice tasty glass of good port.

COMEDIAN: Right...all together now...See if the boys
can drown out the girls...One...Two...Three...

(They launch into the song once again. Blackout.
Lights on Scene Three.)

Scene Three SUNDAY, 26th JULY, 1914

Moray's house. Afternoon.

RALPH is standing by the window. MORAY is at the table, sheets of paper in front of him, working out something.

MORAY: It's a hell of a lot of flour, Ralphie! Getting shot of all that flour! Nearly half a shipload!

RALPH: We're buying just at the right time, Moray! This war with Austria and Serbia's already pushing up prices...The way things are going, we could sell two shiploads at the price we're paying!

MORAY: Ralphie, we should be fighting to stop this war spreading, man! Never mind rushing to get a bloody stake in it!

RALPH: I know, Moray...I know!

MORAY: We should be working to turn it into a war for Socialism, man!

RALPH: I've been up at nights, Moray! Trying to come to some decision...Francis was nearly getting the doctor, the other night...She thought I had a temperature...I was sweating all night...

MORAY: I don't think I did you or the movement a good turn, bringing you and Fanny together...

RALPH: I wish Foster would never have approached me! I wish I'd paid for those pianos, weeks ago! And I'd never have had the capital to be able to even think about it...

MORAY: Mind...She wasn't as bad, before she was married...You can't blame us altogether...

RALPH: Francis is a gem, Moray...You've no idea! She's a gem!

MORAY: God! A thousand quid each!...What about the Germans, Ralphie? What happens if the Germans start shouting for their cash for the pianos?

RALPH: With all this international trouble, I can hold off paying for months...We could sell two shiploads by that time.

MORAY: A <u>thousand quid</u>! Christ! That would set us up for life!

RALPH: It's not just this one deal, Moray...We're getting into this market just at the right time. We'll form a company...The three of us directors...

MORAY: Turn ourselves into Capitalists!

RALPH: We're just distributing, Moray...You couldn't say we're directly exploiting labour...

MORAY: Those pianos...The German bosses have already paid the German workers for their labour in making them. You're not stealing anything from the German workers, even if you never paid for them.

RALPH: Absolutely, Moray...

MORAY: Engels had a factory...

RALPH: Now Engels <u>was</u> a Capitalist, Moray...

MORAY: If Engels would have given up his factory, Marx would never have been able to write Das Kapital...It's a dirty world, Ralphie! Capitalism's turned it into a bloody shithouse! You're bound to get your hands dirty, if you want to clean it up!

RALPH: And the point is, Moray: if we don't take up this offer, somebody else will...All <u>we</u> want out of it is a fair profit...But if somebody ruthless got hold of it...

MORAY: Looka! We're both tarred with the one brush! We're realists. We face the facts of life! It's alright for those bloody purists, sitting on their arses, playing at revolution! But we <u>work</u> at it! We have to bear the real brunt of the revolution! We've got all the bloody back-breaking work...The suffering... Being pulled twenty different ways at the same time!

This could be a new way to Socialism, Ralphie! A completely new strategy! If enough Socialists got control of business...

RALPH: I can see the situation much clearer now, Moray...My mind's much lighter...It's a wonderful instrument the dialectic!

MORAY (looking into the mirror above the fireplace... studying himself): Mind...There's always the chance we might be kidding ourselves...We could be... Definitely...

RALPH: I don't follow you, Moray?

MORAY: I mean <u>kidding</u> ourselves, man! We're bloody
traitors to Socialism – but we're blinding ourselves
with reason that we're not...It's easy enough...
Isn't it?

RALPH (worried): I can't see that we're doing anything
like that, Moray, can you?

MORAY: I've got a wife and four kids, Ralphie...
You've got a wife and a half and three...

RALPH: We've got a lot of responsibilities, Moray.

MORAY: Christ! You don't know the half of it, Ralphie!

RALPH: I think we've looked at this problem pretty
honestly...(Appealing to MORAY) Don't you, Moray?

MORAY: Looka, Ralphie...I see this thousand quid and
a business of my own...In touching distance...I
need the money, Ralphie...We'd be bloody daft not to
grab what God or luck's dropped to us...Socialism
needs us, man...What's good for us, can't be all that
bloody bad for Socialism, can it?

END OF SCENE

WORKING CLASS MOVEMENTS

Lights on the music–hall stage. Two COMEDIANS enter, carrying their rostrums. On one of the rostrums: 'Dr Shotton's lively laxatives for daily regularity', on the other: 'Workers of the world! Now is the hour! You have controlled yourself long enough'. They both begin their spiels.

POLITICIAN: I have come here today, friends, to tell you what is wrong with the working class movements.

SALESMAN: In six cases out of ten, they are not regular.

POLITICIAN: Too often have we seen the capitalist class going through their characteristic motions!

SALESMAN: In six cases out of ten only with great difficulty!

POLITICIAN: The people refuse to be kept in ignorance any longer about what exactly goes on in the privacy of the Government closets!

SALESMAN: And Dr Shotton, after ten years of study, has at last discovered the secret.

POLITICIAN: Friends, I say this to you. We must have action, more action and more action.

SALESMAN: One tablespoon a day of Dr Shotton's lively laxative is all that's needed.

POLITICIAN: The working–class are not going to stand for this any longer!

(Blackout. Lights on Scene Four.)

Scene Four

Moray's house. The family have descended yet again on MORAY.

MORAY: I've been going away for weeks...Everybody knows I've been going away for weeks.

ANNIE: Eee...If I had a baby to be christened! I'd put off anything for it! I'd put off anything to see it christened and set on the right road!

MARGARET: Annie...Do you know what was running through me mind, the other day...That Jew man Aa used to work for...

FRANCIS: Moray Bell! Reverend Harrison came round specially to see me.

ANNIE: What were you saying about the Jew man, Margaret?

FRANCIS: Wait a minute, Annie! We're trying to get this christening settled!

MORAY: It's my son...But he comes round to you! That's logical, isn't it? That's the typical logic of the clergy.

MARGARET (to ANNIE): It was just running in me mind, Annie...It might be that dog Georgie bought you when you were first married...

GEORGE: Ye want to stand by yer guns, Moray, Man. Ye divvent want te mess aboot we' bloody christenin's on Bank Holiday weekend!

RAY: George Willis! Will you keep out of this!

ANNIE: Georgie!

MORAY: The lad's thriving, Fannie...He's taking no hurt that he's still waiting for God to put his stamp on his name...

FRANCIS: He came round to me specially...He knows you, Moray...And your ideas...He's been very concerned about the poor little thing being denied its rights as a Christian, just because of your wild ideas...

ANNIE: Wait a minute, Francis...I just want to know what the Jew man told Margaret...

MORAY: He's not a Christian, yet...And pouring holy water over the bugger is not going to make him one, either!

RAY: Margaret...It's not holy water...We're not Catholics...Moray...

MORAY: It's a bit late in the day to come to you about the christening, isn't it...

ANNIE: What about the dog, Margaret?

MARGARET: That's right...He said Jews when they get married...Never take in any pets...Till after the first child.

ANNIE: What happens if you take a pet...

GEORGE: What would you call a pet, Maggie...A budgie? Would a pigeon be a pet...If you kept him in the yard?

MARGARET: I don't know how it works...Exactly... But if you take a pet in...It's supposed to stop you having babies...You know what funny people the Jews are...

GEORGE: Eee...If taking a pet in's the way to stop you having babies...The bloody pet shops would make a bloody fortune, man.

ANNIE: George...Watch your tongue, will you...

GEORGE: That's good, isn't it...Ralph. Taking a cat into the house to stop you having kids...

MARGARET: There's no doubt about it, they're funny people Jews...

FRANCIS: I think it was very good of him...To come over specially to tell us he had a vacancy for Moray...

ANNIE: Do you think there's anything in it, Margaret?

MARGARET: Eee...Aa don't know, Annie...

ANNIE: Fannie...You didn't have any pets before you had Jackie...Moray hadn't before he had Joyce... Nor Ray...

GEORGE: We didn't get the dog till we were two months married, man!

RAY: I think that's a perfect time for a christening. Bank Holiday Sunday...You couldn't get a better!

MORAY: Harrison has four christenings, already, Ray...That'll keep God happy for that week. He doesn't want to do everybody at the one shot. There'll be God, the next Sunday, getting used to all them christenings...And there'll be bugger all for him. Harrison'll have doused them all in one big blow out!

FRANCIS: As it happens, it's turned out Reverend Harrison's has only two christenings...One of the babies he was supposed to have christened went down with inflammation of the lung...And the other... There's something wrong with it...

MARGARET: Did it die?

RAY: It passed away.

MORAY: I've got me plans made now, Fanny...It should've passed away earlier.

FRANCIS: Sometimes, I doubt if you're all there, Moray Bell. I do!

MARGARET: Fanny...Aa wouldn't feel happy with that Sunday...What with Moray going and paintin' the kitchen green...And little Moray takin' the place of a dead child...Aa wouldn't feel right...Havin' him christened like that...

FRANCIS: He's taking nobody's place. You've got a funny way of looking at things, at times, Margaret! Little Moray's taking nobody's place.

RAY: There just happens to be a vacancy.

MORAY: Looka...My arrangements are made now...I'm expected in London...

GEORGE: What Aa divvent understand is ye spendin' all that money on fares an' wastin' a good holiday week-end just to bloody march for Ireland...If that bloody Irish can't fight for their own bloody country, that's their pigeon, isn't it? What's bloody Ireland got te de with ye, Moray, man? Ye're a bloody Tynesider!

MORAY: It's not only the peace of Ireland we're fighting for now, Georgie, man...It's the peace of Europe...

ANNIE: Eee. Moray...If there was a war all of a sudden ...With this trouble in Serbia...While you were in London...

MORAY: There's not going to be any war, Annie, man!

RAY: The way things are just now...Anything could happen...

ANNIE: And Margaret left all on her own with the children! Eee, Moray...You're surely not going to leave them at a time like this!

MORAY: Annie, there's not going to be a war...The people are on the rise...

GEORGE: Grey's got a trick or two up his sleeve... Aa've got me money on Grey...Grey's a gentleman! He's a perfect gentleman! Aa challenge anybody te deny it!

MORAY: Georgie...Do _you_ fancy a war, just now?

GEORGE: What are ye talkin' aboot, man? What the hell would Aa want with a bloody war!

MORAY: We're done fighting Capitalist wars, aren't we, Georgie...

GEORGE: Aa'm tellin' ye, Moray, man...Grey's me man! And there's nothin' wrong with Asquith, either. He's a canny chap, Asquith...Aa've got nothin' against him!

MORAY: We're done fighting the Capitalists' wars! The people would rise to a man and overthrow any government that tried to lead them into one!

FRANCIS: Moray Bell! Would you get down to earth! Reverend Harrison has said he'll be happy to christen little Moray next Sunday...

MORAY (dismissing it): It's too short notice.

FRANCIS: It's nothing of the kind. It's not too short notice, at all!

RAY: All the family's here.

FRANCIS: We're not going to make a big affair.

RAY: We'll all help to make the tea...

MORAY (dismissing it absolutely, once and for all): I've told you! It's too short notice! That's final!

FRANCIS: Look here Moray Bell...Don't think because you've got yourself a good job, selling groceries for Pattersons...you can go about dictating like that! If it wasn't for me and Ralph...You wouldn't be where you are, just now...You'd still be a twopence-halfpenny clerk in Andersons...

RAY: Don't think you've changed all that much from the old days when you were wetting your bed years after you'd started school...

ANNIE: Remember what they used to call him...Ee...
It was terrible...

GEORGE: What did they used to call you Morrie?

FRANCIS: It was you that started it, Annie...

ANNIE: It was not...I don't know who it was.

GEORGE: What did they used to call him Annie man?

ANNIE: Eee...Don't ask us, George...Don't ask us...

MORAY: They called us...the Pisser, George...When-
ever I was lost or something...Me Mam used to say
...Where's the Pisser...

MARGARET: Moray.

MORAY: I'm just telling him what they called us.

RAY: Till he was nearly ten and all Maggie.

MORAY: I had a weak bladder.

ANNIE: In the winter, it was terrible...You'd walk
into his bedroom...

GEORGE: Aa was never a bed wetter...None of me
family were...There were ten in the family...and
not one...

FRANCIS: I was just bringing him down to size...That's
what you all of you need from time to time.

RAY: They're all the same...You've got to give them a
big knock now and then to remind them who they are.

MORAY: You've reminded us now, Fannie! You've got
us down now – I'm The Pisser...

The two COMEDIANS are playing the KAISER and his AIDE.

KAISER: The Cochin–Chinese Embassy in Berlin has sent out a letter with my stamp upside down. Such an act of aggression cannot be allowed to go unpunished. Declare war on them.

(AIDE clicks his heels.)

KAISER: The budgie who did its business on my portrait in the National Gallery came from Africa. This is a deliberate act of provocation. Declare war immediately.

(AIDE clicks his heels.)

KAISER: You can serve tea now...

(They throw off their hats and roles and launch into the song.)

SONG:
How does the Kaiser drink 'is tea,
Please tell me please,
How does dear old Kaiser Bill
Drink it up and'ave his fill.
'Ow does the Kaiser 'ave 'is cheerin' cup,
'Ow does he fill it up
'Ow does the Kaiser drink his tea,
Please tell me, please.

The Captain takes a spoon of the best,
From eighteen carat Lipton's chest.
The General gets it nice and hot,
The Major General pours it into the pot.
The Field Marshall lets it stew,
Till he gets the perfect brew.
The Empress pours it out
The Kaiser puts it down 'is spout.
That's the way,
That's the way,
The Kaiser drinks 'is tea.

How does the Kaiser eat 'is bangers and mash,
Please tell me please,
Does he like his skins all crisp and brown,
Does he spread it with butter to help them down.
Does he stick his bangers in his mash,

Or chop them all up in a nice brown hash,
How does the Kaiser have his bangers and mash,
Please tell me please.

There's a General standin' on his right,
With his bangers on a plate,
And another with a big black 'tash,
With his gravy and his mash,
When the Kaiser yells: Right, now, Bob.
The General stuffs his bangers down his gob.
Then the bloke with the big black tash
Shovels in the gravy and the mash,
That's the way,
That's the way,
The Kaiser has his bangers and his mash.

What happens when the Kaiser goes to bed at night,
Please tell me please,
When he slides right under his sheets at night
Does he cuddle and hug his heart's delight.
Does he do the same as you and me,
Is he full of fun and fancy free,
What happens when the Kaiser goes to bed at night.
Please, tell me, please.

Just at the foot of his bed,
There's twenty guardsman dressed in red,
They're the biggest in the land –
Just in case the Kaiser might need a bit of an 'and.
And while the Kaiser and his missus lie,
They all shout 'Ushabye!'
That's the way, That's the way,
A Kaiser sleeps at night.

That's the way, Yes, that's the way,
The Kaiser sleeps at night...

(They both dance out on their last lines. Coda orchestra as lights on for Scene Five.)

Scene Five   TUESDAY, 28th JULY, 1914

The platform of a public hall. Early evening.

FLORRIE and MORAY are preparing for the evening's
meeting, arranging leaflets and pinning up various hopeful
slogans:

'Serbian and Austrian Labour against Serbian and Austrian Capital - not Serbian Labour against Austrian Labour!'

'No more Capitalist butchery and plunder'

'The next war - a war for Socialism'

'British workers have nothing to do with the Serbo/ Austrian Capitalists' dispute!' etc. etc.

MORAY is subdued and distant from FLORRIE. He is hiding himself from her in his work. FLORRIE is aware of this. She turns to him.

FLORRIE: Moray...Are you sure you want to go away for the Bank Holiday?

MORAY: It was my idea, man! Yes...I want to go away ...We've got the cottage booked and everything...

FLORRIE (going towards him. Trying to bring him back to her again): Do you know what I'm going to do, Moray? I'm going to pull you out of bed while it's still dark. Just before dawn. And drag you up to the top of Cheviot to see the sun rising. Will that be nice, Moray?

MORAY (turning away to pin up a poster. Avoiding contact): I'd just as soon let it catch us rising, Florrie! (He catches her disappointment at his reaction...and tries to make up for it.) I like the Cheviots...I like following the streams right up to the top...

FLORRIE: I wish you were as light as me, Moray! If you had the one attache case like us...Instead of all that luggage!

MORAY: Florrie, love! It'll be alright...It'll be alright man! Looka...You get nowt for nowt in this world, Florrie...You know that...You only draw out what you pay for...

FLORRIE: Ee, I wish I knew you, Moray...Just a bit, Moray...I wish I knew you...

MORAY: Florrie you know us...All there's worth knowing...

FLORRIE: It's so hard to know anybody! Why should it be so hard to know people? I know nothing about you, Moray...I don't, Moray, love...You hide from us all the time...

MORAY: Honestly, man...There's nowt to know...This is me...This is all there is...

FLORRIE: You leaving the children and Margaret over the holidays...I can't believe it's that easy for you ...I mean...Things like that...

MORAY: It was my idea, wasn't it? Going away and –

FLORRIE: Leaving the children on their own over the holidays...and Margaret...

MORAY: Florrie...You don't know Maggie...You don't know what she's like...Maggie just exists...She just struggles on...She just exists, man...I've never her seen her enjoy anything...She thinks there's something wrong enjoying yourself. It's a sin! If she's having a good time...It must be a sin ...She never sits down and has a meal with us... She doesn't even like to be caught enjoying her dinner...That's all she does, Florrie...She just exists...

FLORRIE: She's never had a chance to do anything else, has she?

MORAY: How have you had a chance...How have I had a chance?

FLORRIE: She's just like millions of other people... They never get a chance to do anything else except exist...That's what we're supposed to be fighting for, isn't it? To give people a chance to grow and live...

MORAY: I'll tell you what gets us, Florrie...Having to make up stories and lies for the girls...That's a bugger, Florrie! When you love them...And you've to feed them stories and lies...

(They both work for a few moments, without speaking.)

FLORRIE: Am I worth it all, Moray? Am I? Are you? Ee...I don't know...I don't know, Moray...I love you...I do...I love you, Moray...But...I want it to be nice...and happy...I don't want to be involved in crying...and tears...and getting sad...

MORAY (putting his arms round her): It'll be alright, Love...I won't let you get sad...

FLORRIE (breaking away from him): We've got too much to do, just now, Moray! This is the turning

point...We should be pushing with all our might...
The door's nearly open...We're nearly through...

MORAY (indicating the posters): We're pushing, aren't
we?

FLORRIE: We haven't any time to be sad...and sorry
for ourselves...

MORAY: I'm not sorry for myself. Are you? Are you
sorry for yourself?

FLORRIE: No. I'm not sorry for myself.

MORAY: This is part of the revolution, you and me...
That's the way I see it.

FLORRIE: Is it?

MORAY: You and me. That's part of the revolution.
Marriages of true minds...

FLORRIE: Maybe I am sorry for myself...Why couldn't
I have fallen in love with a nice, single man. With
just an attache-case like me...

MORAY: Florrie, I'm telling you...You only draw out
what you've paid in...Maggie and me...That's not
a marriage, is it?

FLORRIE: Isn't it? It must have been sometimes...
You've got children...

MORAY: It's no example for my children, is it? A life-
less marriage like that...

FLORRIE: I don't know, Moray...Probably not...I
don't know.

    ·(She begins to arrange a pile of leaflets. MORAY
    looks at the posters...then at the speaker's table.)

MORAY: There's me on that platform...Spouting on
what should be done to save the world...What the
government should do...How they should run the
country...How the world should be run...And I'm
right...I know...We're right, Florrie...How is
it so easy to understand big things like that...like
running the country...and the world...And it's so
hard to understand your own life?

FLORRIE(taking his hands): Moray, You love us...
That's why you go with us...I love you...That's
why I go with you...That's the ground, isn't it...
Everything stands on that...

MORAY: Yes...It does...That's the ground, Florrie...

FLORRIE (teasing him): What you have to do, Moray, is start with the simple things in life...Government... and world politics...and peace...and war...And once you've mastered them...Then you can go on to people...See?

MORAY: You're a bitch, aren't you, Florrie?

FLORRIE: I've a good clear mind...Even my father admits it...'Ye have a good clear mind, lass... Ye've a mind more like a man's than a lass's...'

<u>END OF SCENE</u>

6 CLOSING NUMBER OF THE FIRST
PART OF THE SHOW

POLLY, dressed as a male impersonator, enters to
the cheers of the audience, followed by the COMEDIANS
and the rest of the bill. In the audience, GEORGE, un-
able to restrain himself, has jumped up and is cheering
her. ANNIE pulls him down...POLLY smiles in his
direction and launches into the first verse of 'Let's
all go down the Strand'.

The company join in the chorus. The second chorus
takes on a military form. The company line up and
mark time as they whistle a chorus. Then they all
suddenly launch into the words again...cheers and
shouts as the first half ends...GEORGE yelling and
waving his cap: 'More! More! More!'

(Blackout.)

Scene Six   WEDNESDAY, 29th JULY, 1914

Moray's house.

MARGARET at the sink, washing. MORAY is reading by
the fire. Baby sleeping in its cot.

MARGARET: No...I know a <u>windy</u> smile, Moray...He
gave us a real smile...Just like yours. Just like a
real wee Moray!

MORAY: That's advanced for him, isn't it? Smiling at
that age.

MARGARET: Helen smiled at his age...I think...You
forget, don't you? You forget what they were when
they were babies...

(MORAY watches her at her work. He moves over
to her. Forcing himself to try and make some contact with her.)

MORAY: Do you think most women are like you, Maggie?
When they get married...They've got their children
and their cooking and their housework and their
washing...There's no room in their minds for
anything else...

MARGARET: And looking after their men...

MORAY: I'm tryin' to remember what you were like when we were first married...

MARGARET: What else do you want us to have on me mind, Moray?

MORAY: I'm just trying to think on. What did we talk about when we were courting and when we were first married?

MARGARET: What are you bringing all that up for, just now, Moray? That's years ago!

MORAY: We went walks...And to theatres...

MARGARET: You sometimes took us to meetings...About Dreadnoughts...and Socialism...One about Morocco ...or something...

MORAY: That's right! Did you have room in your mind for things like that, then?

MARGARET: You're funny, them days, Moray...You're acting funny...

MORAY: Do you remember the Boer War? What did you make of the Boer War, Maggie?

MARGARET: Aa was just a girl, Moray, man...

MORAY: What did you make of it?

MARGARET: Aa don't like any war....People killing each other...

MORAY: That's the right position, Maggie...Against all wars!

MARGARET: Anyway...If anything happens...With that flour and sugar you got us, Moray...we won't starve, anyway, Moray...

MORAY: You soon stopped going to meetings with us... After you were married...I remember, now...

MARGARET: Helen was on top of us, before we knew it, Moray...And then the other two...

MORAY: We hadn't the people behind us, then...That was what went wrong with the Boer War...If we'd had the people behind us then like we have now...We'd soon've stopped it!

MARGARET: Anyway...We've got flour and sugar and potatoes in...

MORAY: Do you not think the people can stop a war, Maggie? Do you not think the people can stop a war, now?

MARGARET: Ee, Aa don't know, Moray...I don't know anything about them things...

MORAY: Maggie...Have you ever tried saying to us exactly what you think?

MARGARET: Moray...Aa don't know anything about them things Aa'm telling you!

MORAY: Are you frightened, Maggie? Are you frightened of saying what you think to us?

MAGGIE: I'm yer wife, man! You're daft! Why should I be frightened of you, Moray! Ee, some of the things you come out with!

MORAY: You don't think we can stop being pulled into this war, Maggie?

MAGGIE: Aa don't want us to get into this war, Moray... You know that...You sent away to the army... Zeppelins comin' over and maimin' the children... Aa don't want anything like that...Aa'd be not right in the head if Aa did, wouldn't Aa...But Aa don't understand what's happening, Moray. If the Germans or the Austrians or the French are going to attack us...Have we not to stop them? You see, Aa don't understand what's going –

MORAY: Nobody's going to attack us...Nobody's threatened to attack us. Some people would like to see this country getting mixed up in this Austrian war... But not because anybody's going to attack us... Because it's good for business...They'll sell more guns and bullets...and warships...and make some more conquests...You understand, Maggie?

MARGARET (bored, a little now): Yes.

MORAY: That's the only reason we'd go to war. It's simple enough, isn't it, Maggie?

MARGARET: When the children are grown up, Moray ...And Aa have some time to meself...Aa'll be able to think more about them things...

MORAY: It's a straightforward, clear issue...Isn't it?

MARGARET: Yes...We'll go out more together, then... Moray...Aa'll maybe start going to meetings with you again...And we'll go out to the Music Hall or to see a play at least once a week, eh, Moray?

MORAY: Just say what you think, Maggie? Do you not think it's as simple as that?

MARGARET: I'm saying what I think, Moray...

MORAY: What do you think, then? What other reason would we get involved in this war for?

MARGARET: We're miles away from London, here, Moray...How do we know what's going on there... In the minds of the people in the Government...and that...Aa don't even know sometimes what goes on between the family...Aa don't even know what goes on in _your_ mind, Moray!

MORAY: Maggie...It's _you_ that does the hiding from us...It's _you_ that's always done the hiding, Maggie...

MARGARET: Aa've never stopped you going to your meetings, Moray...Being away all day Sundays... Aa've never said anything to stop you...

MORAY: You didn't say anything about us going off for the Bank Holiday...You're against us going, but, Maggie,...You're disappointed I'm not staying with you...

MARGARET: Aa'm disappointed for the children's sake. The children see little enough of you, as it is.

MORAY: What about you, Maggie? You don't see much of us either, do you?

MARGARET: It doesn't matter about me. It matters about the children.

MORAY: How doesn't it matter about you, man? (She applies herself to her washing, ignoring him) How doesn't it matter about you, man?

MARGARET (turning on him): Does it, Moray? Does it matter to you, Moray? Whatever Aa'd say, ye'd still go away for the Bank Holiday...

MORAY: But if you'd've said it, man! If ye'd've come out with it...

MARGARET: You're going to London for the Bank Holiday weekend, Moray. It's settled...Aa'm not going to fight with ye about it...

MORAY: Do you think I'm wasting my time, Maggie? (She ignores him) It upsets us, Maggie...Never having enough time to play with the girls...And go out with them...Do you know that?

MARGARET: Aa know ye love them...Aa know that...

MORAY: Do you not think I can do anything to stop this war? If it's coming, it'll come...Nothing I can do will stop it.

MARGARET: I don't know, Moray...Mebbes you can...

MORAY: But if I can't...If I'm wasting my time...If I can do bugger all! Christ! That's a terrible thing, Maggie...God, man! That's a right bugger! All that time I was shouting on my platform, making bloody speeches, giving out leaflets...I could've been with my children...I've ended up with nothing...I've thrown away the happiness of being with my children ...I've denied them my company...for nothing! For bugger all! (As he is speaking, the baby begins to cry) Is that what you were thinking, Maggie? Is that how your mind was running? (MARGARET is listening to the baby, not hearing him) Maggie...Maggie!

MARGARET: Ee! That's Moray wantin' his last feed, already...And Aa haven't got halfway through me wash! (Drying her hands) Aa'm comin', Moray... Aa'm comin' now, honey!

MORAY (blocked): Tommie, Maggie!...Tommie! Not bloody Moray!

(But MAGGIE has gone to her crying baby.)

END OF SCENE

Epilogue

Lights on the body of the ARCHDUKE lying in state. The
Emperor FRANZ JOSEPH steps forward and lays a wreath
at the foot of the coffin, watched by the KAISER. He turns
to address the audience over the body.

FRANZ JOSEPH: The Royal Government of Austria/Hungary,
  not having given a satisfactory reply by the Royal Government of Servia to its note presented by the Austrian/
  Hungarian minister in Belgrade, finds it necessary
  to safeguard its right and interests and have recourse
  for the purpose to force of arms. (He bows to the
  KAISER. The KAISER returns the bow) Austria/Hungary
  therefore, considers itself from this moment in a
  state of war with Serbia.

(He takes a lightened taper and lights one of the four
candles at each corner of the coffin. Curtain down.
Lights up on the stage as the orchestra plays 'Let's
all go down the Strand' for the intermission.)

<u>END OF ACT ONE</u>

ACT TWO

Prologue

Lights on the body of the Archduke.

Russia, France and Great Britain confront the KAISER and the Emperor FRANZ JOSEPH over the body.

SASSANOV (Russia): Austria is looking for some pretext to gobble up Serbia. Next she will go on to Bulgaria. And then we shall have Austria on the Black Sea, threatening the very life-blood of Russia. If Austria persists on this course. In that case, we shall have no alternative. Russia will make war on Germany.

(The KAISER looks at FRANCE.)

VIVIANI (France): It is now clear, in the light of the German ultimatum to Russia to halt mobilisation, that France herself is threatened with a German invasion. We are at present virtually undefended. Germany could enter France at this moment without a shot. Every day's delay in mobilisation means a twenty kilometre loss of territory. France has therefore no alternative but to issue a call for General Mobilisation.

(The KAISER turns to ENGLAND.)

GREY (England): Austria has declared war on Serbia and is at this moment bombarding Belgrade. If the conflict remains confined to Austria and Russia, Britain would probably continue to be neutral. But if Germany and France should be drawn into the conflict, the situation would be immediately altered. In that event...(He bows to the KAISER)...It would not be practicable to stand aside and wait for any length of time.

(The five men stand in their two blocks on either side of the corpse...immovable.)

(Blackout. Lights on Act Two.)

POLLY enters in her bathing-costume with the rest
of the company. The COMEDIANS are busy with their
telescopes, spying on the girls. POLLY launches into
the first verse:

POLLY:
    Every one delights to spend their summer holiday
    Down beside the side of the silvery sea.
    I'm no exception to the rule – in fact, if I'd my way,
    I'd reside by the side of the silvery sea.
    But when you're the common-or-garden Smith or
    Jones or Brown,
    As Business up in town, you've got to settle down.
    You save up all the money you can till summer comes
    around,
    Then away you go to a spot you know
    Where the cockleshells are found.

CHORUS:
    Oh, I do like to be beside the seaside,
    I do like to be beside the sea.
    I do like a stroll upon the prom, prom, prom,
    Where the brass bands play tiddley-om-pom-pom.
    So just let me be beside the seaside
    I'll be beside myself with glee,
    And there's lots of boys beside, I should like to be
    beside,
    Beside the seaside, beside the sea.

(The COMEDIANS come forward with their telescopes
and sing a verse of 'All the girls are lovely by the
Seaside.')

COMEDIANS:
    All the girls are lovely by the seaside,
    All the girls are lovely by the sea.
    When they're strolling down beside the ocean,
    The ocean – what a commotion.
    All the girls are lovely by the seaside
    With their curls and bits of drapery.
    Flighty Flo and Giddy Gert
    Each one quite a saucy flirt.
    With their figures nice and pert,
    Tucked inside a hobble skirt,

Wearing a blouse you know for cert
Was made from father's flannel – vest,
They're all lovely by the sea.

(Everybody launches into a final chorus of 'I do
like to be beside the Seaside.')

(Blackout. Lights on Act Two, Scene One.)

Scene One   THURSDAY, 30th JULY, 1914

The Pollocks' evening

STAN is sitting by the fire, pouring himself out a dose
of his white–mixture. The girls, ROSE and MAY, are
trimming a hat...trying it on each other to see how it
looks...The door is thrown open and MARY backs into
the room, pulling at some piece of furniture...BARNEY
is at the other end. They succeed in getting it through
the door – it's a new sideboard. STAN stands up, his
medicine bottle in one hand, making some impotent
gesture to help.

MARY: Move out the way a minute, man...Are you just
    going to sit there with your white mixture...

    (STAN gets up.)

MARY: We've wheeled that all the way from Clara
    Street...

BARNEY: Is your man bad?

STAN: Could you not have waited till Saturday after-
    noon...I'd've helped you...

MARY: In the daylight...That's the kind of thing you
    would do...Wheel furniture in the broad daylight all
    the way from Clara Street to Leazes Road.

BARNEY: Do you think he'll like it?

MARY: Jesus...He'd better like...I'll not wheel it
    all the way back...

BARNEY: It's a lovely piece of furniture...It could make
    the centrepiece of your room...

MARY: What do you think of it, then? Is that not a beau-
    tiful piece...

STAN: It's canny...

ROSE: It's a bit dark, Ma, isn't it...

BARNEY: It's class, miss. All the gentry are going in for the dark stuff just now.

MARY: May, get the kettle on. Give Mr Norry a cup of tea...Sit down Mr Norry...Rest your legs a minute. This white mixture my man's taking...He's been taking it since he was a boy...His mother used to give him it.

BARNEY: Is that a fact...

MARY: That's Mr Norry's sideboard...

NORRIE: I'm moving house.

MARY: His wife has gone back to her parents.

NORRIE: We never got on...from the beginning...

MARY: We never got on from the beginning either. But we're still hanging on here like grim death (To STAN) Is your stomach bad?

STAN: Aa've got a touch of heartburn. That's all.

MARY(to BARNEY): He's had it since he was a lad.

STAN: Aa was born with a sensitive stomach.

MARY: It's all that holy water and fish they have. (Going over to admire the sideboard) It's a beautiful bit of furniture, that...

BARNEY: It sets off yer whole room.

MARY: Mr Norrie says the same as me. All those countries up in arms.

BARNEY: It all started with Ireland.

MARY: They're all acting under the secret instructions of the Pope. First of all the Irish Catholics rose.

STAN: What about the bloody Irish Protestants? They've been doing their share, too, haven't they?

MARY: Then you have the Austrians and the Russians and the Serbïans...The Pope is making a bid for world power.

ROSE: Ma...Don't be daft...The Pope's for peace...

BARNEY: That's what he says...But he's up there in the Vatican makin' cannon balls like hot cakes...For other folk to fire!

MARY: The priests are for peace...They were preaching

about peace in the church last Sunday...

(BARNEY is trying to work this out...He's obviously got himself into a nest of Catholics.)

MARY: Me two daughters are Catholic, Mr Norrie...
And me man...

BARNEY (retreating): Aa'm very sorry if Aa said anythin' out of place...Aa was talkin' generally, like
...Aa've got nothing personally against –

MARY: You're just speaking the truth, man. You never
need to apologise for speaking the truth! Everybody
knows the Catholics are out for dominating the world.
And a sorry world it'll be if they succeed... (To
STAN) Have you had your dinner?

BARNEY: Aa always say there's good and bad everywhere...

STAN: No...Aa haven't had me dinner. Me stomach's
upset, man!

BARNEY: Catholic and Protestant.

MARY: No bloody wonder yer stomach's upset...Sitting
there drinking that bloody rubbish. (To BARNEY)
He goes over to Tynemouth every Saturday to get a
bottle...He was born in Tynemouth...

BARNEY (rising): Well...Aa'll be on me way.

STAN: Looka, man...They're bloody Protestants in
Germany...They're behind the whole bloody business
...Yer German Protestants.

BARNEY (waving his cap): Aa'll be away, then, missus...

MARY: That's right...It's up to Germany to stand up
against the Pope...and all them Catholics in Russia...

BARNEY (going while the going's good): A good night
to ye all.

ROSE: The Pope's nothing to do with Russian Catholics...

MARY: That's a Catholic for you...They'd talk themselves out of their own funerals...

STAN: They're Greek Catholics, man, in Russia...

MARY: Aa don't care if they're bloody Chinese Catholics.
They're all the same breed...Tarred with the Pope's
brush.

MAY: Going to the Olympia, Ma...We saw our Florrie's

lad...

ROSE: Man, more like it...You can hardly call him a
 lad...

MARY: Are you trouble-making again, May?

ROSE: She's not trouble-making...We're just telling
 you something...Florrie's man had two little girls
 with him...

MAY: Holding his hand.

ROSE: On either side of him...

MAY: Lovely little girls...

ROSE: They might have been his nieces or a friends'
 maybe. I'm not saying they weren't...

ROSE: But the way he was going on with them...He
 looked as if he was very attached to them.

STAN: What ages were they?

MAY: Oh, one was maybe about four...The other six.

STAN: Aa've told you all along...That Communist
 company she's been mixing with...

MARY: Are you going to have your supper?

STAN: Aa'll take it...Aa don't want good food wasted...

MARY: It won't go to waste...Aa'll share it with you...
 Aa'm a bit hungry...After all that heavy work.

STAN: I wouldn't put it past them Socialists, Mary...
 That's the way they go on...All that free love and
 carrying on with women.

ROSE: He looked as if he was very attached to them.

MARY: Florrie's going about with a married man...?

MAY: No...Ma...I - We didn't say that...

MARY: We might as well face up to the blackest it could
 be...What have you got to say about it, Stan? Sitting
 there, with your white mixture on your right hand
 and your supper on your left...

STAN: Mary, man...I feel bad, man...Aa've taken over
 all weak...Mary...

MARY: You'd better get your father a bottle...And we'll
 put him to bed...

ROSE: He definitely looks a canny age...Ma...At least
 thirty...

STAN: Aa knew something like this was going to happen
to Florrie...Mary...She's been shaping that way...
since she left school. She's been shaping that way
...She's got no religion behind her...She's turned
her back on God and Christ...and everything...

MAY: We've just got her word for it that she's going to
London...haven't we...

STAN: The next thing, she'll be having a child with
him...If she's not already got one...The Lord
forbid...

MARY: You can go to the Chapel in the morning, and see
if the Pope can do anything to keep her off having a
baby...

STAN: Mary...I don't understand the way your mind
works...I've never been able to fathom the way
your mind goes on...Mary...Aa'd got such strong
hopes for me lasses, Mary, man...Aa wanted them
to have nice weddings, with canny lads...In good
positions...See them all set up...

MARY: Looka, Stan, honey...What can you do...If
you'd've been another kind of father...You would've
given her a good hiding...Locked her in the house
...But you're not the kind of man, are you Stan?

STAN: Aa've never lifted me hand to any of them...
Never...Aa've always closed my eyes whenever you
did...

MARY: And if you were that kind of man...And the
feelings were strong enough in her...You'd only
drive her from the house anyway, in the end...

ROSE: She's been acting funny for a long time, Ma...

MAY: I've noticed it. She's been on her high horse
for months...

ROSE: As if she had anything to be on her high horse
about...If he is...

MARY: Rose, May...Looka...She's your sister, girls
...It could have been just as easy either of you...

STAN: The Lord forbid...

ROSE: Ma!

MARY: Easier! Because after it was all over...All
you'd have to do was go into the box...And you'd be
washed whiter than you were born...

STAN: Are you going to tackle her...or will I?

MARY: What would you say to her...You tackle her,
Stan. You go upstairs and carve away at your dog,
or something...Just calm yourself a bit...And you
both get in the kitchen, and dry the dishes or something...or get to bed.

(Girls go out.)

STAN: What are we going to do Mary...?

MARY: Stan...I don't know...Florrie's a good girl,
Stan...She's one of those capable people...Even now
...I don't know what it is...But I feel I can trust her
to look after herself...I've always felt that...with
her...I've never felt it about the other two...

STAN: We've got to do something to knock it on the head
...We might still be in time...No harm'll be done.

MARY: It's still not sure he is married...

STAN: He is, man...Aa can feel it...Aa was worried
about it all the time...

MARY: She's not going about worried looking...or
strained...

STAN: But what about those two little girls...If they're
his...And their mother...

MARY: The trouble is...I can see her doing something
exactly like that...If she looked up to a man...There's
not many men I can see her going with...Can you?

STAN: Eee...Aa don't know Mary...Aa divvent knaa...

MARY: You get to bed, Stan...I'll try and get her
speaking about it...You don't upset yourself about
it...She's a capable girl...She can look after herself
...Whatever happens, she'll fall on her feet...

END OF SCENE

PRACTICAL SOCIALISM

The POLITICIAN is finishing his speech to his AUDIENCE of one.

POLITICIAN: That is the real meaning of Socialism. To share what we have with our fellow men. That is the real road to happiness.

(Climbs down from his soap-box. The AUDIENCE approaches him.)

AUDIENCE: This sharing business. You say I should share what I've got with my fellow men?

POLITICIAN: That's right, my friend.

AUDIENCE: That'll make me happy?

POLITICIAN: Absolutely. How much have you got?

AUDIENCE: I've got fourteen quid. You share with me – and I'll share with you. Is that the idea?

POLITICIAN: You've obviously listened very carefully to my words...You've grasped the whole idea, my friend...There you are...I've got six pounds... Half of that is three...which is yours...You have fourteen...Half of that's seven...which is mine...

(Taking the seven from his AUDIENCE. The AUDIENCE counts his money...Not at all happy at the result of his first experiment in Socialism...he has ten pounds for fourteen.)

POLITICIAN: Don't you feel much happier, now.

AUDIENCE: Well, to tell you the truth...I don't...No ...I don't think I'll bother, thank you...You give me back my seven quid –

POLITICIAN: Wait a minute...Wait a minute...You've got the wrong idea...You've made me happier... You've made your fellow man happier...That's what makes you happy...

AUDIENCE: That's how it works...I see...But I'm the one who's doing the best deal here...Because I'm going to be much happier than you because I've made you much happier...Trick, isn't it...?

POLITICIAN: Well...Good luck to you, my friend...I'm delighted to have put you on the road to Socialism. (He goes.)

(A PASSER-BY approaches AUDIENCE. The AUDIENCE turns to him.)

AUDIENCE: Excuse me...Do you fancy a bit of Socialism, just now...To pass the time of day away...and make you happier...

PASSER-BY: Share and share alike? That kind of thing?

AUDIENCE: That's the idea. I've got a tenner. How have you?

PASSER-BY: I've got two pounds.

AUDIENCE: Right...I give you half of my tenner...five quid...You give me half of your two...A quid...

PASSER-BY: Pleasure!

AUDIENCE: Do you feel happier?

PASSER-BY (looking at his six quid): Much happier.

AUDIENCE: That's because you've made your fellow man happy. Makes you happy.

PASSER-BY (going): Oh...I see how it works...Thanks for the tip!

(AUDIENCE looks at his money...counts it. Stares at his six pounds, dejected. The POLITICIAN passes by again. He stops him as he is about to pass.)

AUDIENCE: Here. This Socialism lark...It's not working ...I started with fourteen quid...I've done two Socialist deals...and I'm down to six...It's not making us feel at all happy...I can tell you!

POLITICIAN: No...I can see exactly what's happened... You've been dealing with people poorer than yourself... (As he is speaking a GENTLEMAN approaches.) What you want to do is find someone better off than you. That's the whole idea. The rich sharing with the poor ...Look...That gentleman over there with the Gold Albert...That's the kind of person you want to practise your Socialism with.

AUDIENCE (looking at the GENT): Yes...He looks pretty well off, doesn't he...I'll tackle him. (Goes over to the GENT.)

AUDIENCE (to GENT): Excuse me, sir, would you be interested in trying out a bit of Socialism to make you happy?

GENT: Share and share alike...Eh? That kind of thing? Yes...Try anything once...Why not? I've got forty pounds on me...How much have you?

AUDIENCE (winking at POLITICIAN): I've got six...

GENT (bringing out his money): Right...I give you twenty ...you give me twenty...You give me your six...I give you your share of the six...Good day!

(All done very quickly, – like a conjuror doing a trick. He walks off before the AUDIENCE can say anything. He is left holding his three notes...The POLITICIAN comes over to him and grabs the notes.)

AUDIENCE: Hey! What's that for?

POLITICIAN: That's your subscription to the party.

(Blackout. Lights on Scene Two.)

Scene Two FRIDAY 31st JULY, 1914

Moray's house. A crisis.

ANNIE: Eee...I can't believe it Maggie! I can't believe it...It's like a dream...The whole thing's like a dream!

FRANCIS: I've known for weeks something's been going on. He's had a funny look about him...

RAY: It's the crowd he's been mixing with...They're all the same...I've heard stories about these Clarion Girls! They're a fast crowd...

FRANCIS: And he just came out with it? Just like that...?

MARGARET: Fanny...He's not himself...He was very upset...He was crying.

WALTER: He wants to bloody cry and all!

RAY: He does, too, Walter!

ANNIE: What made him come out with it!

FRANCIS: How long has he been going about with her?

MARGARET: She's nearly half his age...

RAY: I think you're quite right Maggie...He's not all there...

RAY: He was always a funny lad...

FRANCIS: Not that way...but...

ANNIE: No...He wasn't that way...

WALTER: I'd tackle him meself...Maggie's me only sister...

MARGARET: Walter...Please...I've got enough to worry us without you and him coming to blows...

WALTER: That's what would happen...We'd bloody well come to blows...Aa'd bash him...

FRANCIS: He'd deserve it...He would deserve everything you gave him...

RAY: I can understand well how you must feel, Walter... Deserting your sister...

MARGARET: Ray...He didn't say he was going to desert us...He was crying. He promised us he'd never leave us short...He'd always look after the children...

WALTER: But it's me trade...If I did anything to me hands...I've got nothing to fall back on...

MARGARET: That's Walter's life...his piano...

WALTER: It's me livelihood and me life...

ANNIE: You've got a beautiful touch, Walter...I've always said, you've got a beautiful touch. Sometimes when I go to the Majestic I forget about the picture just listening to you...

WALTER: I would bash him up in a minute...That's what he wants a bloody good hiding...

MARGARET: Walter...That's not going to do any good ...That's not going to do any good...

ANNIE: It's that Socialist crowd man...They've turned his head...

FRANCIS: He's never been the same since they made him Chairman of that Socialist lot...They're a bad lot... You can see what they're like...The way the women go about...They're worse than prostitutes...

ANNIE: At least prostitutes do it because that's the only way they can keep body and soul together...

FRANCIS: If that was the only way I could keep body and soul together...

ANNIE: No Fannie...I mean...to say...You can understand...

FRANCIS: I would shoot myself...I would shoot myself... I'd do myself in...

RAY: I would too...

FRANCIS: But they're even worse than prostitutes...

MARGARET: Breaking up a happy marriage like that... What kind of woman can she be...You can imagine what kind of woman she is...

ANNIE: What did he say Maggie...Did he give you any reason...?

MARGARET: I've been a good wife to him, and a good mother to his children. I don't think anybody can say I've not...

FRANCIS: You've been a lovely wife...a lovely wife Maggie...and a good mother...You couldn't get better...You've got those girls like they were the daughters of lords you have...Hasn't she...?

MARGARET: He said exactly the same thing...He says I've been a good wife...and a good mother...

RAY: The man's off his head...He doesn't know where he is...What is he leaving you for then?

MARGARET: I don't know Ray...I don't understand anything...

ANNIE: He never bothered with girls when he was a lad ...Did he Fannie...We always used to tease him... Didn't we...

FRANCIS: Maggie was his first girl...That was maybe the trouble...He should've maybe dallied about a bit before he met Maggie, and we wouldn't't've had this trouble we've got today.

RAY: The man's nearly forty...What is he thinking of running after young girls...

FRANCIS: It's a bit late in the day, to be sowing your wild oats?

RAY: She'd be running after him more likely...I know those man-mad fast women...She'd be chasing him ...She's turned his head...

MAGGIE: That's exactly what she's done, Fannie...
She's turned his head...

ANNIE: He says you're a good wife...

MARGARET: He's got nothing against us...He likes us...
He likes us...That's what he said...Maggie...I like
you...I think you're a lovely person...I do...

RAY: I don't understand it...I've never heard of anything like it in my life...Have you ever heard of anything like that in your life...He thinks you're a
lovely person.

WALTER: You see...It's like this...I'm a family man...

MARGARET: Walter...It's alright honey...I know...

WALTER: No...I'm explaining to your sisters in law
...I've got four children, and another on the way...

ANNIE: Ee...I didn't know Muriel was expecting again
...That's lovely...When is it due Walter?

WALTER: October...sometime...What I'm saying is if
I was single...I would take him by the scruff of the
neck...

ANNIE: Walter...Your hands are tied...You can't do
anything...

MARGARET: He says he wants us to stay friends...
There's no reason he says why we shouldn't stay
friends...

FRANCIS: The man's mad...The man doesn't know what
he's talking about...

RAY: He wants you to stay friends...

MARGARET: He says his first duty is to give us all
enough money not to be short...

WALTER: I should bloody hope so...

FRANCIS: Maggie...You should bleed him...You should
skin him alive...You should get every penny you can
out of him...

RAY: Squeeze him dry...

FRANCIS: You don't want to leave a penny for that filthy
rotten prostitute...

WALTER: I've told her...She's to see her lawyer...
She's to see a lawyer straight away...

MARGARET: Walter...I don't want a lawyer...I want me man...Man...I want me children's father...

WALTER: Looka man...You want to see a lawyer I'll go down with you...

ANNIE: What lovely children he has...Does he not realise that...How lucky he is having four lovely children...

RAY: Moray's not a month old Maggie...Does he realise what he's doing...thinking of leaving you with a month old baby...

FRANCIS: He won't leave her...We'll make sure he doesn't ...We're not going to let him off like that...I've got some say...I'm the oldest in the family...Maybe Mother and Father are dead and they're not there any longer to keep on the right lines...But we're here...

ANNIE: Eee it's a good job Fanny Ma and Da didn't live to see this...

RAY: It would've killed them...Wouldn't it...

WALTER: It's a good job our Mother and Father have passed away...

RAY: I don't know what would've happened. It would've broken their hearts...

ANNIE: Ma...always expected Moray to be a big man... They gave him all that schooling...They got him fixed up in the railway...

RAY: They liked Maggie...Da always had a soft spot in his heart for Maggie...

WALTER: Well...Let's be honest...He mebbes liked her in the end...

FRANCIS: That's what happens in the best of families Walter. It sometimes takes the in-laws a bit to get used to their daughters in law...

WALTER: Your Mother didn't give Maggie an easy time...

MARGARET: Walter...This isn't the time for casting –

WALTER: No...It just came up...And I'm just saying we all know Maggie wasn't given all that good a welcome into the Bell's at first...Mr and Mrs Bell were hoping for better things of Moray...

FRANCIS: Walter...No mother ever thinks her daughter in law is good enough for her son...

RAY: They both liked her in the end...They were always coming to see her and the children...

ANNIE: Eee...If they were alive today...

FRANCIS: If they were alive today it would never happen ...It's since Moray hadn't anybody to steady him and control he's gone wild...

RAY: He likes you...and he thinks you're a lovely person...What is he running away from...?

FRANCIS: What he wants is two wives...I can see it exactly...I know him...He wants his cake and he wants to eat it...I can see exactly what's running through his twisted mind...

ANNIE: For them to live together...Under the same roof ...Eee...Fannie...

FRANCIS: That's what he'd like if he could get away with it...

RAY: That's what comes of not having any religion or rules to go by...

ANNIE: Where's he going to get the money to keep two wives...

FRANCIS: That's what I'm talking about...If he's beyond reason...Then we'll have to take a stick to him

MARGARET: Fannie...I don't want him hurt...I don't want him driven to anything...He's in a terrible state ...He might do something to himself...

FRANCIS: He'll do nothing to himself...He's too fond of himself that one!

END OF SCENE

TALENT SPOT

Lights on Music Hall. The MASTER OF CEREMONIES is
standing waiting for the first volunteer in the night's
talent spot.

MC: Come, ladies and gentlemen...I'm sure there must
be countless talented ladies and gents in the audience.
This is your spot on the bill. Step forward, now,
please...Any lady or gent with vocal, instrumental,
comic or terpsichorean talent...

(A struggle is going on in the pit. GEORGE is trying
to stand up, ANNIE is pulling him down. Eventually
he breaks clear and climbs on to the stage...amid the
cheers and applause of the audience. He's obviously
been working overtime in the bar during the interval.
He announces his song.)

GEORGE: Paganini – 'The Pitman's Frolic'. (Bends
down to the conductor) In D...

(The orchestra plays a chord...GEORGE goes into
his song.)

GEORGE:
Come, lift up your lugs and Aa'll give ye a song,
It's none of the best, but it's braw, new and funny,
In these weary times when we're not varry thrang,
A stave cheers wor hearts, though it gives us no money.
We left Shiney Row, to Newcassell did steer,
Wi' three or four more of wor neighbours so canny,
Determined te gan te the Playhouse te hear,
The King of Aal fiddlers, the great
Baggy-Nanny.

Ta-ra-ra -ra-ra-ra -ra-ra-ra-ra-ra-ra; ra
Ra-ra; -ra-ra-ra-ra-ra-ra.

We got to the door, in the crowd we did crush,
Half way up the stairs, Aa was carried se handy,
The lassie behind us cried: 'Push, hinny, push!
Till they squeezed me as small and as smart as a dandy.
The curtain flew up, and a lady did squall,
To fine music played by a cockney bit manny,
Then from the front stalls, Aa soon heard me friends
bawl:

Hats off, smash yer brains! Here comes great Baggy-Nanny!

Ta-ra-ra etc.

Scene Three   SATURDAY, 1st AUGUST, 1914

Ralph's office.

MORAY is studying some papers. RALPH is watching him.

MORAY: That was a bit of a mouthful from Fannie, there, wasn't it?

(RALPH hands him a paper.)

RALPH: That's a copy of the delivery schedule...

MORAY: Where do you stand, Ralphie? You kept yourself well out of things, there, didn't you?

RALPH: I've got other things on my mind, just now, Moray. The whole International's collapsing...They were all there...Keir Hardie...Luxemburg...Kautsky ...And they could do nothing!

MORAY: And we get this invitation from the Government on top of it all! What do you want to do about it, Ralphie? Put in a tender?

RALPH: We're campaigning against this war spreading ...I can't see how we can go ahead and supply the troops and at the same time carry on with our campaign against the war.

MORAY: Can we supply? Can we get hold of enough flour to supply?

RALPH: We can supply. I've checked. That's not the point, but, is it, Moray?

MORAY: Looka...We're going to come up against problems like this all the time, man! We're hammering out a new line of action...We're breaking new ground ...We're not selling guns or shells or even coal for bloody battleships...It's just bread for the troops ...For the workers...Somebody's got to feed the poor buggers!

RALPH: Yes...It's only flour...The trouble is there's so much smoke around, just now...You can't see anything clearly...

MORAY: Ralphie...Where <u>do</u> you stand with me and this girl?

RALPH: That's your business, isn't it, Moray...Your personal problem...

MORAY: Ralphie...I like you, man...You need a real mate at times, Ralphie...It's a bugger if all you've got to turn to is a woman, all the time! I like you, Ralphie, man! But you're nobody's mate, are you? You're nobody's mate, Ralphie!

RALPH: What difference does it make, what I think about this, Moray?

MORAY: Bugger all. It makes bugger all difference!

RALPH: It's bad for the movement. That's my reaction. (MORAY waits for something more intimate, something deeper.) We're fighting to win the trust and the confidence of the people, Moray...Things like this... They don't do us any good...

MORAY: You could never see yourself doing anything like that, Ralph?

RALPH: Socialism is facing up to the truth. What's the most important – your own self-satisfaction – or winning the revolution?

MORAY: And this flour deal...

RALPH: Yes. This flour deal...Somebody will supply – if we don't...

MORAY: You want us to work out a theory for you to help yourself and the revolution at the same time, Ralphie?

RALPH: I'm just pointing out there'll be no shortages of bids for the contract, Moray...

MORAY: Marx says you've got to learn to use history... You've got to learn to turn history against the ruling classes...If it turns out we can't do anything to stop this war spreading...That's not a failure...I don't reckon that failure...

RALPH: I don't want any excuses for ourselves, Moray... If it's wrong...It's wrong...

MORAY: I'm working out something, man! What I reckon is a failure is the Austrian Socialists, throwing up their hands and giving it all up...Or the German

Socialists ready to vote for war credits...If we didn't turn this war into a war against Capitalism, Ralphie ...That would be a bloody failure, alright! When we get a situation like this...Ripe for changes...All the bloody structures toppling down...And we do bugger all to make sure our structures aren't set up in their place...That would be a failure alright!

RALPH: The point is, <u>somebody</u> will supply the troops.

MORAY: It's going to make bugger all difference if we supply or we don't...Apart from putting a few hundred quid in our pockets...

RALPH: Out of which we'll put a percentage into the movement...

MORAY (half laughing at him...half serious): There you are, Ralphie! We're putting Marx's golden words into action! Exactly as he wrote them. 'The Government will be financing their own destruction. The Capitalists are selling us the rope to hang them with!'

<u>END OF SCENE</u>

The ladies army is being marched on to parade for the morning inspection by Major POLLY.

MAJOR: Sergeant Brown!

SERGEANT: Madame!

MAJOR: Those frills round the field guns. They clash.

SERGEANT: Yes, madame...

MAJOR: Pinks and red and blues and greens all mixed together...Clashing horribly...Put it right.

SERGEANT: Yes, Madame!

MAJOR: Private Wallace. (She hides behind sombody else.) Private Wallace!

PRIVATE: Present, Madame!

MAJOR: I thought I told you to use the rose patterned wallpaper for the trenches...and the lilac for the forward dugouts...(WALLACE cries.) There's no need to get upset about it...I was just as disappointed....I'd set my heart on the rose patterns for the trenches...

PRIVATE (sniffling): I thought...

MAJOR: Speak up, will you, Private Wallace...

PRIVATE: I thought the lilac went so nice with the green lino...(Breaking down.) I was trying my best...With all those shells...And shooting...(The MAJOR puts an arm round her...comforting her.)

MAJOR: Now, Mavis...Don't take on so like that...I'll tell you what to do...You go to the Company hairdressers and have your hair nicely done...And have a nice cup of tea...And if you'd like...Go over to Supplies and tell them I said you were to have a new uniform...

PRIVATE: You don't think it looks awful, the lilac and green...?

MAJOR: No...You run along to the hairdressers, now... (She turns to the rest of the company) Just one final word, girls...I do realise that sometimes you are

called out at all hours of the night to battle...And
I know how hard it is to look one's best at three
o'clock in the morning. But it doesn't take a moment
to put on a little face powder...and a touch of lip-
stick...We are trying to uphold the good name of
our sex...(As she is speaking, there is a loud ex-
plosion) Now...What's happened now!

(Private WALLACE comes running up.)

PRIVATE: It's Peggy, Madame...She must have brassoed
the shells in the armoury too hard...The whole
ammunition dump has gone up!

(Blackout. Lights on Scene Four.)

Scene Four   SUNDAY, 2nd AUGUST, 1914

The Pollock's house...afternoon.

MARY and FLORRIE are alone...MARY is painting a chair
...FLORRIE is fixing her hair and getting ready to go out.

MARY: Wilkinson's gave us half a stone of flour yester-
day. Did I tell you, Florrie?

FLORRIE: I thought I'd get you some in town, Ma...But
there were queues all over...Some of the shops were
even closed...

MARY: Half a stone won't last us long...Not the way your
Da puts down his bread!

FLORRIE: I might be able to get some for you...Ma...
I'll try...

MARY (probing): You changed your mind quick about going
away for the weekend, didn't you, Florrie?

FLORRIE: There's plenty campaigning to be done here, Ma
...Without us going away...

MARY: You had your case packed and everything...

FLORRIE: Did you fix the hem in me pink dress, Ma...?

MARY: I did! I never let anybody down. If everybody in
this family carried out their responsibilities like me,
it would be a happier thirty-five Clara Street!

FLORRIE: There's a flower show in the Spanish City
tomorrow, Ma...

MARY: But I've only myself to blame, getting involved with the faith in the first place! What else can you expect from them? It's that lazy, Irish, Catholic bloody. Comes from all them years sitting in their mud huts, with their potatoes and holy water and pigs by the fire! It would make anybody's bloody lazy, that carry on! No bloody wonder they've got no backbone to them!

FLORRIE: Why don't you get Da to take you to the Flower Show Ma...And you could have a picnic on the beach, after...

MARY: I'll have me usual depressing, miserable Bank Holiday! Your Da'll make sure about that. Don't worry about me, Florrie! Anyway, I care nothing for flower-shows...All them flowers together...Like a bloody funeral!

FLORRIE (kissing her): Ma...You're a daft brush at times ...aren't you?

(MARY concentrating on her painting. From time to time she looks up to watch FLORRIE...FLORRIE is dressing her hair with much care and attention...)

MARY (feeling her way. Trying to be as light and casual as she can): I saw your friend the other night, Florrie ...(FLORRIE continues brushing her hair) I just happened to pass the meeting...and this fellow was speaking...And I had a feeling...That's him...One of the men round the platform told us...That was his name...Moray...Moray Bell...

FLORRIE (trying to be calm): That's funny, Ma, isn't it?

MARY: You know how you sometimes get that feeling about something...I just knew that was him... (Continues her painting...FLORRIE says nothing) Eee. I'm not sure about that colour, Florrie, are you? I told him I wanted egg-shell blue. That's not egg-shell blue, is it? Would you call that egg-shell blue, Florrie?

FLORRIE: I like it, Ma.

MARY: I care nowt for it! It's got no body to it...It's insipid...I'll finish painting it...And if I've enough money left over next week I'll buy some white...A nice hard white...(Continues to paint) He's not a Catholic, is he, Florrie?

FLORRIE: He's nothing...like me...His Family's C of E if that makes any difference.

MARY: That's something to be thankful for, anyway! He
didn't look like one...I can always tell them! They've
got that wild, Irish, hunted look about them!...There's
a bedroom-suite in the window in Henderson's, Florrie
...Not far from here...Clifton Road...I was thinking
of going along after I'd finished this to have a look at
it...

FLORRIE: You could do with a new dressing-table, Ma...

MARY: I was thinking for your room, Florrie...I was
looking at your room this morning...It's not a bedroom
for a young girl...That chest of drawers belonged to
me Mam's Mam!

FLORRIE: Ma...You know what Rose and May are like! If
you changed my room and didn't do anything about
their's!

MARY: There's two wardrobes...I could give them one
of them...

FLORRIE: Ma...You don't want to go to any expense over
us...I like my bedroom...It's lovely...Honest, Ma...
I like it...

MARY: You won't be leaving us for a bit, yet, love...
A girl needs a nice room for herself...There's no
harm in going along to have a look at it...(Waiting for
some response from FLORRIE) Is there?

FLORRIE: No...Do you like me hair like this, Ma?

MARY: You look lovely, lass...You're a lovely lass...
You could get any man, a lass like you...

FLORRIE (looking in the mirror): It's a change, anyway...

MARY: Moray Bell's a married man, Florrie.

FLORRIE: Yes, Ma...That's right.

MARY: Did he tell you?

FLORRIE: I knew the first time I met him.

MARY: Florrie...I'm not much of a mother to you, love
...I know...I'm a funny kind of mother...I stood
there, listening to him speaking...Taking him in...
Another mother would've torn the shirt off his back!
I just stood there...Looking at him...

FLORRIE: He's a good speaker, Ma...Isn't he?

MARY: The way he speaks...His soft...quiet voice. He

looks such a lovely, nice fellow...If anybody said
to you. That man there. Married with young children
...He's messing about with a single girl...You'd
never believe them!

FLORRIE: He didn't go after me, Ma...It was just the
way it happened...I didn't go after him...We just
came together...

MARY: I just can't understand it, Florrie! It's beyond
us! You've always been a good girl, Florrie, love
...You've always had a lovely nature...And to look
at him...He's a gentleman...The way he was speaking
...You could see...He had a good nature...He was
a lovely man...Not to look at...He's nothing much
to look at...But inside him...I just can't fathom it,
Florrie...It's beyond us...

FLORRIE (putting her arm round her): Ma...Don't get
yourself upset about it...It'll be alright...Don't
worry about it, Ma...It'll be alright...

MARY: The whole thing's beyond us, Florrie...On my
first night with your Da...I stayed up all night...
I was frightened to go into bed with him! And I loved
him! God only knows what fate made us fall in love
with a priest-ridden red hot Catholic like your Da
...But I loved him...

FLORRIE: We haven't made up our minds about anything yet, Ma...Honest, Ma...We haven't decided
what we'll do...

MARY: Do you think you might live with him Florrie?
Would you go away and live with him?

FLORRIE: I might, Ma...Yes...If that's what we decided...Yes...Ma.

MARY: Eee...I just can't understand it, Florrie, love.
Never mind the disgrace and the shame! These poor
children he'd be leaving! They'd be on me mind
night and day, Florrie...! I could never stop thinking
about them!

FLORRIE: He's not going to desert the children, Ma...
I wouldn't let him...He couldn't do it, Ma...I
wouldn't look at him if he did!

MARY: Eee...The deeper I get into it the less I understand it!

FLORRIE: Ma, I'm telling you...Don't worry yourself
about us...It's too hard for you to cope with, Ma,

this...You'll only get yourself upset, for nothing,
Ma...It's not as bad as it looks through your eyes,
Ma...We can cope with it, Ma...Honest...If we do
go away...He'll still look after the children...
Taking them out and –

MARY: Florrie, love...This isn't one of your socialist
fairy-tales! This is the lives of real people you're
talking about, honey! People touching you, Florrie!
Are you hearing yourself when you speak, love? Do
you understand what you're saying? He's going to go
from one wife to the other – back and forward!

FLORRIE: Ma...We're trying to build a new world...a
healthy world, Ma...A real world, Ma...Not a
fairy-tale world...All these laws and rules and
commandments...They've just been made up, Ma...
They're the fairy-tales!

MARY: Does he not love his children? Has he no love
for his children?

FLORRIE: He's a good father. He's a lovely father. He
is...He maybe loves them too much...

MARY: He looks a good father. I thought he was. You
can tell...Florrie, love...I don't know where I am!
There's no unravelling this! I don't know how to help
you! I   don't know what to do for the best! I've always
been like that! I've never been much use as a mother
...I've never been a good, strong mother like me
mother!

FLORRIE: Ma...You're a lovely mother...You've always
been a lovely mother to us...You couldn't be better,
Ma...

MARY (overcome...looking at her chair): Eee...I don't
know what to do! Do you think I should leave it...
It looks better when it's all done...

FLORRIE: It's nice, Ma...It's a lovely blue...

MARY (taking FLORRIE'S hand): It just wasn't in me,
Florrie...I've never liked laying down the law to you
...It wouldn't have been so bad if your Da had been a
bit stronger...

FLORRIE: Ma...I can look after myself...You know that,
Ma...

MARY (looking at her): I hope so, lass...I hope to dear
God you can!

END OF SCENE

11 <u>THE LATEST RAGTIME SENSATION</u> <u>FROM AMERICA</u>

The company sing and perform the sensation –
'Alexander's Ragtime Band'.

(Blackout. Lights on Scene Five.)

Scene Five   MONDAY, 3rd AUGUST, 1914

Corner of a pub. MORAY and GEORGE are playing darts.

GEORGE: Twelve and a tanner a fortnight and wor coal,
Moray, man! Aa'd be bloody daft not to grab at that.
And wor army pay on top of it all!

MORAY: Who pays the twelve-and-six? The company?

GEORGE: Colonel Simpson, man. It's comin' out of his
pocket...If there's a war, he wants the first volun-
teers to come from his pit...

MORAY: For Christ's sake, man...You're not thinking
of volunteering! You'd be fighting against your comrades,man! German and Austrian fellow workers...
Some of them pitmen, like you...

GEORGE: Aa fancy a bit of a jaunt te France...Or the
Continent.

MORAY: You'll fancy it alright when you get a bloody
bayonet up your backside!

GEORGE: Tell ye, man...It can't be much worse than
eighteen inches at the Brockwell...With water pourin'
down the bloody face the whole shift!

MORAY: Georgie...The Government's bloody spoiling
to get us into this war...They've got to get into it
...If there's going to be a fight between the Capitalists of Europe for a new division of the spoils of
the world, the British Capitalists are going to make
bloody sure they're not going to be left out of it.
Looka, man...Let the Government declare war on
Germany and Austria and who the hell else they want.
Let them wave their bloody revolvers and shout

'advance!' But for Christ's sake...Make bloody sure
nobody's behind them to obey their stupid bloody orders!
Leave them bloody standing there while we go out to
build a new peaceful world. Georgie, man...Show
them up for the daft stupid bastards they are!

GEORGE: Moray, man...Aa'm a pitman...Aa's a hewer
...If Asquith came down the pit and started to tell
us how te gan about cuttin' a seam, Aa'd sharp
bloody tell him where to get off...Gentleman though
he may be...(MORAY is about to interrupt) No, man
...Let us finish, Moray, man...The same as he has
every right to tell us where te bloody get off if Aa
came round to Downing Street to tell him how te run
the country...That's his trade...and that's mine...
That's what we're paying him for...Aa'm not bein'
paid te sit up aal neet to work out the rights and
wrongs between Serbia and Italy...and Germany and
Russia...The men that run this country...They're
bred to it...They're educated to it from the cradle,
Moray, man...

MORAY: George, the whole of Europe's going to be at
each others' throats, man! The whole world's going
to be set on fire Georgie...Christ, man! Is that what
you call running a country, getting involved in that!
Is that knowin' yer trade as a pitman bringing the
whole bloody seam down on top of you!

GEORGE: Looka...We've done a lot of hard bloody graft
and hard bloody fightin' te get te where we are today,
Moray...Ye just want us te stand back and let the
bloody Kaiser grab it all from us?

MORAY: Where are we, today, Georgie? Where are you,
Georgie?

GEORGE: They're gannin' te trample over Belgium,
aren't they? They're gannin' te march right through
Belgium...Aa've never liked a bully!

MORAY: Aa'm asking you, Georgie, where are you?
after all the hard graftin' and the hard fighting, where
are you today? Just now...with the Minimum Wage
Act still running, you've just enough to keep you and
Annie...What happens when it runs out next March,
Georgie?

GEORGE: Looka, Moray...Can ye de bloody better? Can
ye run the country better? Ye've got yerself in a
canny bloody mess, haven't ye?

MORAY: Christ, Georgie, man...You're not bloody
starting on that, now?

GEORGE: Moray...Ye could run it through the whole of the chorus at the bloody Palace, if ye're lucky enough! It's your bloody business...It's bugger aal to de with me...Aa wouldn't mind a lass on the side meself, at times, if Aa could get one...Ye bugger ye! Gettin' yerself a young lass like that!

MORAY: Is that why you're running off to France, you Tory bastard, you!

GEORGE: Aa'm tellin' ye, Moray...There's some lasses ye see in the street, them days...Ye can hardly keep yer bloody hands off them! But Christ, ye bugger. Aa'd keep it to meself! Aa wouldn't bloody climb te the top of Grey's monument and shout it out te aal bloody Newcastle!

MORAY: I want to marry this girl, Georgie...She's my real match...Can you understand, Georgie?

GEORGE: Maggie's a canny woman, Moray...She keeps yer bairns and yer house lovely...And she's bonny looking on top of it all...Christ, man! What more do ye want?

MORAY: What more do you want, Georgie? (GEORGE looks at him, puzzled) Annie's a good wife to you...

GEORGE: She's a lovely wife...Couldn't get a better!

MORAY: Why the hell are you running away from her, then? What are you rushing to volunteer for, man?

GEORGE: Moray...There's gannin' to be a war...Ye can see that, now...Aa'll have te gan some time... If Aa can see Annie a bit more comfortable gannin' when it starts...why the hell shouldn't Aa?

MORAY: You'll be fighting against yourself, Georgie? Against your own class? You're virtually taking a gun and turning it on yourself!

(GEORGE aims for the board...his first two darts are poor shots...he turns at last to MORAY.)

GEORGE: Moray, man...Ye divvent knaa what ye're talkin' aboot! Twelve and a tanner a fortnight and free coal till the end of the war...Is that bloody turnin' a gun on us? Ye divvent knaa what the world's like, man, ye bloody Socialists! Turnin' a gun on meself...Christ! If that's turnin' a gun on meself, Aa'll sharp turn it, ye bugger!

(He throws his last dart...a near bull, this time.)

END OF SCENE

1st COMEDIAN: Mind you. Give credit where credit's due. He's got a lovely big un, the Kaiser has.

2nd COMEDIAN: Not as big as the King's.

1st: Must give him a lot of satisfaction, a nice big un like that! That archduke that got shot...He couldn't have had much of a one.

2nd: Is that how he got shot. Because it wasn't big enough?

1st: Stands to reason, doesn't it? If he'd a big one, and it could stand up to them all...They'd've all been frightened to shoot him, wouldn't they?

2nd: What about the Czar's...You think he's got much of a one.

1st: He might have a big one, alright...You know what them Russians are like...But he doesn't seem to do much with it, does he?

2nd: The Kaiser's must be as fit as a fiddle...All that training and exercise...

1st: Out in all weather...

2nd: But he couldn't beat the King's...

1st: Well...You don't see much of it, do you. He keeps it well hidden...

2nd: It's there...It's waiting there...Whenever he wants to use it...Ready to spring into action...The British Army's the biggest in the world!

(Blackout. Lights on Scene Six.)

Scene Six   TUESDAY, 4th AUGUST, 1914

The town moor. FLORRIE and MORAY have escaped for a moment from the neutrality meeting still going on not far away. From time to time the speeches and the boos and jeers of the crowd reach them.

FLORRIE: It's funny how the larks never get any less on The Moor, isn't it, Moray?

MORAY: More, probably...(A loud burst of jeering reaches them.) We'd've done as much good walking the Cheviots today as trying to move that crowd!

FLORRIE: You'd think with all these cows and sheep around...and people...to tramp on their eggs...It seems daft nesting on the ground...Doesn't it?

MORAY: That shows you there's no master plan made by some God...If there was he'd've made them nest in the trees...Or under the ground...

FLORRIE: But they don't get any less...There's more of them every year...You're right...There is more ...I can't understand that, can you, Moray?

MORAY: Christ! That's the least bloody problem today! Listen to them! Everybody's letting us down. The pitmen...the engineers...the whole bloody working class. The International's collapsing...

FLORRIE: Maybe if you hadn't been so busy with your new flour business, Moray, you might have had more time to save the peace...

MORAY: I'd've had less time, Florrie, man...I'd've done less! Since I started this...and I don't need to worry about money...I'm thinking clearer and clearer every day...My mind's free to worry about the problems that are worth worrying about...

FLORRIE (turning from him): That's fine, then...If you're thinking clearer...

MORAY: Florrie, love, you've got to fight the world as it is, honey...Not as you'd like it to be...If there's a wall in front of you, it's not going to get you anywhere kidding yourself it's not there and trying to walk through it.

(FLORRIE turns to him and looks at him. As if waiting to hear the rest. She stands for some time... without speaking...waiting.)

MORAY: Florrie, I'm on the right road...It's going to be a long and a hard fight, Florrie...We've been kidding ourselves...We're not going to wake up in our new world tomorrow, man...There's no wand to wave to make it rise up, during the night...It's

a harder and longer fight than we thought, Florrie
...We've got to get at this rotten society at the roots
...Looka...I know it, Florrie...I'm on the right
road, man...

FLORRIE: You're on the road for a big villa in Morpeth,
Moray...That's the only road you're on just now...

MORAY: How can you give all you need to give to the
movement if you've always to worry about money?
I'm going to have two families to keep...I've got
to make sure everybody is –

FLORRIE: You don't need to work for me, Moray! I
can work for myself. I don't want any money from you.

MORAY: Florrie, honey...Don't start fighting with us.
Every bugger's fighting with us these days! (FLORRIE
doesn't respond) I love you, man. Don't you turn
against us!

FLORRIE: You love too many people. That's your trouble
Moray. (She turns to him) Moray...Be straight with
us...Don't keep things back from us...That's the
good thing we have...We try and be straight with
each other...You can't help loving your children,
Moray...You don't need to make excuses to us for
loving them...and not going away with us...

MORAY: It wasn't an excuse, man...We'd organised all
those meetings...

FLORRIE: You couldn't leave the children, Moray...
and Margaret...Maybe, you'll never be able to leave
them.

MORAY: Florrie, man! The Germans are in Luxemburg
...They're probably into Belgium by now...(FLORRIE
says nothing) When you've got children...All kinds
of things run through your mind, Florrie...

FLORRIE: It'll happen all the time, Moray...It's bound
to...You can't help it...There's thousands of things
you'll have to keep back from us...Because you think
it'll hurt us...or make us angry...

MORAY: It wasn't just the children, man...We couldn't
run away from all those meetings...It was everything,
Florrie...stopping us going away...It was just the
way it worked out...I had everybody on to us.

FLORRIE: It'll work out again like that...We'll keep
losing each other...I hate it! I hate it, Moray...When

you go off from us like that.

MORAY: Florrie, honey...I'm sorry...It was just...
Everybody was on to us...

FLORRIE: Do you think it'll be like this all the time?

MORAY: It won't be, man...I'll push myself, Florrie
...To hold nothing back from you...

FLORRIE: Moray...How can it not be...I don't like your
new flour business...Or your new theories...It's
just like a kid trying to prove himself in the right...
But I can take them...I can fight honestly with you
about them.

MORAY: And I'll bloody fight you, too –

FLORRIE: But I can't fight honestly about your children
– and Margaret...I've got to be careful there...I've
got to watch what I say...I've got to draw back...

MORAY: For Christ's sake, Florrie, man! This is a
bloody world! You can't get things perfect...

FLORRIE: I want too much, Moray...I know...I want too
much...I can't see myself finding anybody else to love
like I love you.

MORAY (his arm round her): Florrie...We'll be fine...
We'll get a house...in the country...Just outside
Newcastle...The way things are going, I'll have
enough to buy one of them new motor cars...It'll be
alright, love...We'll have a lovely –

FLORRIE: Ee...I wish it would be...I wish I could see
it like that, honey...I'm too selfish, honey...And
too jealous...Come on...We'd better go back and help
the comrades, Moray, love...(She takes his hand...
MORAY says nothing as they walk back to the meeting)
Whatever happens, Moray, I love you...Remember
that...Always remember that, Moray...

END OF SCENE

BY JINGO!

The Palace of Varieties, ever topical, have anticipated events, and are staging a patriotic number. The union jacks have been brought out to wave goodbye to the army leaving Newcastle to fight against the Kaiser.

Stuck for an appropriate war-song, they have had to go back to the Russo-Turkish war for their opening chorus.

'By Jingo'

SONG:
We don't want to fight, but by jingo if we do,
We've got the ships, we've got the men,
And got the money, too.
We've fought and won before, and while we're Britons true,
The Kaiser shan't trample over Belgium.

(A TERRITORIAL moves forward to sing farewell to his sweetheart.)

'The Pitman's Farewell to Newcassell'

CHORUS:
Now, Hinney's Aa'm gannin te leave yes,
King Geordie's asked us te save yes.
Ta-ra, ye canny Tyneside folk,
Din't fash, Aa'll soon be yame.

This German Kaiser Bill, man,
We've had aboot wor fill, man,
He'd like us through the mill, man,
But we'll soon fettle his game.

Ta-ra, me Da and me Mammy,
Me darlin' sweetheart, Fanny,
Remember your dear mannie,
While he's fightin' for his king.

Aa'll make ne mair emotion,
But cross the salt-sea ocean,
Where Aa've a kind of notion,
This war'll soon be done.

(Blackout and fade in the middle of the final chorus and lights on Scene Seven.)

Scene Seven   WEDNESDAY, 5th AUGUST, 1914

Moray's house...Early morning.

MARGARET: It's that paint. Nothing's gone right since you painted the kitchen green!

MORAY: Don't be daft, Maggie, man.

MARGARET: Green's an unlucky colour. Me Mam never touched green...

MORAY: There's nothing lucky or unlucky, Maggie... Everything's in your own hands...

MARGARET: Peggie got her arm scalded...Our Walter's Wendy got the chicken-pox.

MORAY: When things get a bit straightened out, Maggie ...I'll get you a nicer house...With a bit green round you.

MARGARET: I don't want anything from you. Aa want nothing from you!

MORAY: With a nice garden for the children, Maggie ...A garden would make all the difference...

MARGARET: A lot you care about the children! You think the garden'll make up for them not having a father!

MORAY: Maggie...They'll still have their father, man...

MARGARET: Then there was all this war trouble...It's just been one thing after the other. (Turning on him) Aa told you Aa didn't want green! That's the way you've been all the time. You've never done any- thing Aa wanted!

MORAY: Maggie...For Christ's sake, man! I could've painted the walls bloody tartan and the Germans would still be bloody marching on Belgium...The bloody Archduke was shot weeks before Aa bought the paint, man!

MARGARET: Aa'll tell you this: Aa want you to take every one of your belongings out of this house. Aa don't want you to leave a collar stud when you go!

MORAY: I can't leave you just now, Maggie, man...If we get involved in this war...I can't leave you in the middle of all this trouble, Maggie...You never know what can happen...

MARGARET: I should strangle you! I should. I should bloody strangle you!

MORAY: Maggie, I told you...I'll always look after you and the children...You'll be alright, Maggie...

MARGARET: Aa'll never divorce you! Ye can tell your friend that. Aa'll never give her the satisfaction of that! Whatever happens, Aa'll stay your legal wife ...Have you told her that?

MORAY: You could get married again, Maggie...You're just in your prime...You're a good looking woman...

MARGARET (turning on him...absolutely lost): Moray... Aa don't think you're all there! I'm a good looking woman...now! What are you going away for then? I don't think you know where the hell you are! You love your children...I'm a good wife...I'm a good looking woman...And you're desertin' us!

MORAY: I'm not deserting you, Maggie, honey...I'll never desert you!

MAGGIE: What's in your mind, Moray Bell? What kind of daft plan's in your mind, man? Are you going to stop one night here and one night with your friend!

MORAY: They're me children, Maggie...I'm going to look after them...

MARGARET: Is that how you see yourself? Going from the one house to the other! God, I would be bloody daft! To let you back here again after you left us!

MORAY: Don't take it out on the children, Maggie... We've got to make it as easy as we can for the children, Maggie...

MARGARET: There's one way of doing that, isn't there? You're out of your mind, Moray Bell! Coming back-wards and forwards like that! What would Aa tell people? You coming in and out like that...How could Aa hold up me head in front of people...What story could Aa tell Mrs Stephens...and Mrs Curry...? Moray's livin' with his fancy woman...But he's a good Da...He's promised to come in and see his children don't suffer!

MORAY: They're our children, Maggie – not Mrs Curry's or Mrs Stephens'...or any of the other bloody neigh-bours'! You've got to do what you've got to do, Maggie

...You've got to live how you have to live...

MARGARET: Aa don't need you! Aa can look after me own children! We don't need you! If you don't want us — we don't want you!

MORAY: Maggie...The children love us...They need us man...I'm their father...They love their father, Maggie...Looka...In a new house...It'll be easier for you, man...You can make a fresh start...I'll get you a nice house, with a garden...Somewhere where you've —

MARGARET: Big enough to house us all! You and your fancy woman! And me and the children! Is that what you want? We've got to live how we have to live? Is that what your friend thinks too? Does she not bother either, what people think of her? In that case, it won't bother her not being married to you! Never being able to be your wife! (She breaks down) What am Aa going to do? Aa don't know what Aa'm going to do...left on me own with three young children and a baby...Aa don't know what Aa'm going to do... Aa don't know where to turn to! (Crying...)

MORAY (trying to put his arm round her): Maggie... Maggie...honey...

MARGARET (breaking away from him): Get out! Get out, for God's sake...and leave us alone! Get out!

(Impotent, MORAY backs out. MARGARET stands, crying.)

END OF SCENE

Epilogue

The body of the Archduke is still lying in state, the candle lit by Franz Joseph is burning brightly...the other three candles remain unlit.

Across the body the two blocs confront each other – The KAISER and FRANZ JOSEPH – and SASSANOV, VIVIANI and GREY. The KAISER moves forward and turns to RUSSIA.

KAISER: With heavy heart I have been compelled to mobilise my army against a neighbour at whose side it has fought on many a battlefield. With genuine sorrow, do I witness the end of a friendship which Germany loyally has cherished. We draw the sword with a clean conscience and clean hands. Germany is at war with Russia.

(He takes a lighted taper and lights one of the three candles. He turns to FRANCE.)

KAISER: In consequence of French acts of organised hostility and of air attacks on Nuremburg and Karlsruhe, and of the violation by French aviators flying over Belgian territory, the German Empire considers itself in a state of war with France.

(He lights another candle, replaces the taper, and steps back...they all turn to BRITAIN...GREY moves forward.)

GREY: Her Majesty's Government has received no reply to its note to Germany requesting an assurance that the demand made upon Belgium for free passage through Belgian territory will not be proceeded with and that her neutrality will be respected by Germany. The German forces have already violated Belgian territory at Gemminich, near Aix-La-Chapelle and are penetrating still further into Belgium. Consequently – (He takes a lighted taper) We are in a state of war with Germany.

(Instead of touching the remaining unlit candle with his taper, he touches the body, and the coffin bursts into flames. As it burns the lights go on MARGARET... she stands, watching the flames.)

MARGARET: I told him...I pleaded with him...I didn't want that miserable green!

(From a distance the mouth-organ is still playing at the Palace of Varieties...'Tipperary'...as the curtain comes down for

<u>THE END OF THE PLAY</u>